Contents

Editor's Preface   vii

Introduction   1

1 Towards an Interpretative Framework   6
The promise of Marxian approaches   6
The weaknesses of Marxian approaches   11
General features of an interpretative framework   20

**2 The Medieval Cities: The Struggles for
    Domination**   33
Introduction   33
Interpretations   34
The city   37
The patrician city   42
The plebeian city   45
Urban autonomy: rise and fall   46

3 The Emergence of the Modern City   51
Cities and the growth of the modern state   51
From burgher to bourgeois: the rise of a
    capitalist class   56
The triumph of the industrial bourgeoisie   61
Bourgeois domination and legitimacy   66
The rise of organized labour   72
Conclusion   76

4 Bureaucracy, Politics and the City   78
The nature of bureaucratic power   79
Bureaucracy in the ascendant?   83
Bureaucratic power constrained   87
The local and national state   90
The extension of bureaucratic power   93

5 Market Forces and Property Relations   **97**
Introduction   97
The local property owners and the world
  they have lost   99
Property booms and the developers   101
Finance   107
Owner-occupation   111
The role of the state   115

6 Power and Protest in the City   **118**
Changes in social structure   119
Problems of representation   124
Urban politics: issues old and new   128

7 An Agenda for Research   **138**

Notes and References   154

Index   169

THE CITY

PATTERNS OF DOMINATION AND CONFLICT

SOCIOLOGY, POLITICS AND CITIES

Editor: JAMES SIMMIE

PUBLISHED

Manuel Castells: CITY, CLASS AND POWER
Patrick Dunleavy: URBAN POLITICAL ANALYSIS
Brian Elliott and David McCrone: THE CITY
Roger Friedland: POWER AND CRISIS IN THE CITY
John Lambert, Chris Paris and Bob Blackaby: HOUSING POLICY AND THE STATE
James Simmie: POWER, PROPERTY AND CORPORATISM

FORTHCOMING

Valdo Pons and Ray Francis: SLUMS AND SHANTY TOWNS
James Simmie and David Lovatt: MARXISM AND CITIES

The City

Patterns of domination and conflict

BRIAN ELLIOTT AND DAVID McCRONE

Department of Sociology, University of Edinburgh

First published 1982 by
THE MACMILLAN PRESS LTD
London and Basingstoke
Companies and representatives throughout the world

ISBN 0 333 22601 1 (hard cover)
ISBN 0 333 22603 8 (paper cover)

Typeset in Great Britain by
CHROMOSET LIMITED
Shepperton, Middlesex

Printed in Hong Kong

Editor's Preface

Sociology, Politics and Cities

Cities have been the focal points of economic, political and cultural life in all those countries experiencing the kind of rapid industrial and commercial evolution that was first seen in the early nineteenth century in Britain. To understand national economic and political forces was therefore to comprehend the development of cities. To follow culture required insight into urban life. Early appreciations of these links were developed in the German works of Marx, Weber and Simmel.

This early appreciation of the importance of the relationships between national forces and cities was not emphasized in the American analyses of cities stimulated by the Chicago School. Although it was to some extent present in the work of Park, Burgess, McKenzie and Wirth, it was lost in subsequent work which tended to conceptualize cities as isolated and self-contained phenomena. The significance of the relationships between power and cities was, however, kept alive in the American community power study work. The Lynds, Hunter, Dahl and more recently Bachrach, Baratz and Crenson have all made important contributions to our understanding of cities.

The eruption of major urban-located conflicts on both sides of the Atlantic during the 1960s made it quite clear that cities could not be understood within the main American paradigms of the 1920s. They also demonstrated that both national economic forces and the concept of power were central to any comprehension of what was happening in cities at that time.

This intellectual challenge was first met in France in different ways by Lefebvre, Castells and Lojkine. Harvey also made a contribution in Britain. Much of this work was based either on neo-Marxist Althusserian structuralism or on extensions of Marxist political economy, particularly the concept of rent. Although this work provided a great stimulus to urban research, some elements of it have not proved as fruitful as was first hoped. It has suffered from ethnocentricity, circularity, inappropriateness in contemporary circumstances and a lack of comparative empiricism.

A different intellectual response to understanding cities was also started in the late 1960s, this time in Britain, by Rex, Moore and Pahl. They developed some Weberian themes to account for the observable distributions of urban resources by so-called 'gatekeepers'. This type of local work, although useful in understanding local processes, did not address the growing significance of national and international forces in shaping particular urban developments.

The series 'Sociology, Politics and Cities' provides a vehicle for the extension of these debates and for newer contemporary approaches to understanding cities. The series is transdisciplinary, including not only sociological and political work but also interconnected economic and historical research. It includes analyses of both private and public intervention in cities and therefore encompasses an interest in public policy. The main aim of the series is to encourage and stimulate a continuing debate and analysis concerned with capitalist, socialist and underdeveloped cities. It is concerned to develop theoretical understanding of these phenomena based on empirical analyses. On the bases of such understanding the series is also concerned with the formulation and evaluation of significant and relevant urban policies.

London University   JAMES SIMMIE
January 1982

Introduction

Recent events have put 'the city' back on the agenda of public debate. Church leaders and policemen, academics and politicians, community leaders and journalists, all present their diagnoses and solutions to the 'problems' of the cities, and the media convey, day by day, the latest contributions to scholarly or political deliberations about urban affairs. The scenes of skinheads and Asian youths locked in battle, of shops and houses burning or of policemen being stoned and petrol-bombed force a new awareness that all is not well in our towns. The outbreaks of rioting and looting in London or Liverpool or Manchester provide the most recent manifestations of unrest, but the seeds of racial antagonism, of economic frustration or mistrust of police authority have been growing for many years.

For the better part of a decade now, neo-fascist organisations have found it possible to manipulate the resentments against immigrant groups and to mobilize support, principally among white working-class youths, for their reactionary, politically primitive programmes. The decline of inner-city neighbourhoods with decaying housing stock, deserted factories and warehouses, boarded-up stores and diminishing and often impoverished populations, has been in train for a long time. Pockets of so-called 'multiple deprivation' have appeared too in a good many of the large housing estates built during the past thirty years and the misery of life in the high-rise blocks has been with us ever since the planners and the architects and politicians opted for this solution to our housing shortage. Very high concentrations of children and teenagers in public housing areas, a feature of the unbalanced demographic structures encouraged by our building and zoning policies, have frequently led to minor disturbances and the demand for more intensive policing. Coupled with changing police methods, this in turn has led to the growth of much resentment among youngsters in these areas, to a belief that they were kept under surveillance and subject to arbitrary and unjustified arrest. Nourished by political indifference and the spread of unemployment, these seeds bore fruit in outbreaks of collective violence in the summer of 1981.

Among those who were not surprised by these events were many of the social scientists who over the last decade had been involved in what is generally referred to as the 'new urban sociology'; for in their efforts to refurbish this area of the subject, many of them had written about precisely those problems of poverty, inadequate housing, racial conflict and unemployment which provided the triggers for the violence on our streets. Their studies in effect warned governments that the diverse experiences of exclusion, injustice and oppression could lead to such outbursts.

In the 1970s urban sociology in Britain enjoyed something of a revival. Drawing upon an earlier re-orienting of urban studies in France, a comparatively small group of writers succeeded in changing the ways in which urban issues were perceived. To their great credit they forced us to think about housing, planning, community action and a host of other 'stock' issues in a much broader way, linking them to many of the theoretical issues – like the growth of the state or the changing character of capitalist economies – which were prominent in the mainstream of the discipline. Here, as elsewhere, it was Marxist writers who made the running. Urban sociology was revitalized by a resurgence of left-wing scholarship which touched all the social sciences and many traditional 'arts' subjects. Its pervasive influence, together with some of its central tenets, led to a welcome breakdown of the established disciplinary boundaries and urban studies became one part of a sweeping 'political economy'.

This book has to be set against that background of revival and re-orientation. It is a product of the enthusiasm for a new urban sociology, but at the same time is written in order to criticize some aspects of that development and to argue for a greater theoretical permissiveness than has been common during the re-making of that area of study. Specifically, we are trying here, to use some of Max Weber's writings to focus attention on what we see as some neglected issues, to complement, not simply to carp at Marxist approaches. Weber's writing about cities and his more general discussions of power relations deserve to be taken seriously. In the first flush of enthusiasm for the new approach, it was tempting to consign his essay on 'The City' to the sociological attic. It appeared after all to be about medieval, and to a lesser extent, ancient cities and was hard to connect with the kinds of urban settlement that had grown up in the modern period. Certainly to many students it seemed an obscure piece. More generally, as interest in Marxism and especially in the new 'structuralist' Marxism grew, it became easier to dismiss Weber as a 'reactionary' writer and to create a polarity between 'Weberian' sociology and the 'progressive' force of Althusser's Marxism. Few wanted to wear the former label. But to put Weber's books in the attic or to represent his work as simply 'anti-Marxian' is really very foolish. He may have rejected the idea of joining the socialists in the Germany of his day and he may have written about nationalism or about the nature of social science in ways which today meet little approval from liberals or leftists, but still his work remains an extraordinary fertile source of insights and ideas, and his model of interdisciplinary, comparative scholarship something that deserves our respect.

So, in this little volume, we have tried to take from Weber an approach, a perspective in which we can set our studies of urban institutions and structures and the actions and aspirations of their inhabitants. To do that we have had to try to locate the city in history and to pay particular attention to the political as well as economic processes which attended its transformation. Cities can be looked at as concentrations of both political and economic resources and this makes them, now no less than in the medieval period, objects of contention. Today, as always, rulers and their parties want access to and a measure of control over the wealth of cities, over their complexes of manufacture and trade, over their tax revenues, over the opportunities for work and for profit that they offer. More than that, dominant or aspiring classes, governing parties or contenders for power recognize that urban populations can be mobilized for political struggle. Whether it is the medieval princes trying to incorporate the burghers in their systems of rule, or nineteenth-century elites orchestrating 'beer and empire' mobs, or modern parties engineering public displays of support or resistance, the fact is that concentrated urban populations constitute important resources in the contests for power. Weber, more explicitly than Marx, recognized this and his approach invites us to locate urban processes within a wide political framework.

Our brief in this book was to try to develop a distinctive approach, one that differed somewhat from the general lines of work drawing its inspiration from French Marxism of the 1970s. We cannot pretend that the task has been an easy one, for Weber's writing does not constitute a coherent, integrated theory and does not encourage any wholesale rejection of the insights gained by materialist writers. In consequence, the reader will find that we retain a good deal of sympathy for certain Marxist approaches to the understanding of urban development and contemporary life in our cities. Certainly, we find much to commend in the humanistic Marxism of historians like E. P. Thompson or E. Hobsbawm or the Marxisant stance of a sociologist like Charles Tilly. Our purpose then, as it has developed, has become a modest one: to provide criticism of the structuralist variant of Marxism (without doubt the dominant one in the initial re-orienting of urban sociology), to put Weber's essay 'The City' back on the agenda for those concerned with urban studies, but mostly to distil from Weber's general writing an approach which will enable us to perceive cities in a slightly different way thereby attending to some rather neglected issues and pointing the way towards a number of important themes for research.

Our aim throughout has been to provide for those concerned with the problems of our cities an approach which, while it is genuinely sociological – being concerned with the structured regularities of social life, the codes of behaviour, the patterns of belief, the structures of class and status, the web of institutions – is none the less accessible to those in other disciplines. We hope the book will prove of some interest to those in politics, geography and urban planning as well as those in sociology, but we are concerned too that it will not appear so narrowly academic as to deter the interested general reader. To this end, we have tried to write in a plain and simple language, for in our experience many who come to the academic writing of the new urban sociology are rather daunted by the fact that so much seems encoded in an unfamiliar style of discourse.

The book is meant to offer some basis, not merely for the description of urban life, but also for criticism of the economic and political practices and policies that bear on our opportunities as citizens of cities: opportunities for jobs, housing, education and democratic participation. It has been said many times that the task of sociology is criticism but in a period when governments have at their disposal unprecedented capacities for the mobilizing of consensus, and when they often seem, as now, intent on stifling dissent, it is worth reminding ourselves of that commitment. Tom Burns once remarked that 'it is the business of sociologists to conduct a critical debate with the public about its equipment of social institutions'.[1]

The city is a very special human institution (or if you prefer, a complex of institutions). With images of burned-out buildings and police behind their riot shields still fresh in our minds, we must ask some hard questions about what is happening to our urban institutions. What follows is an attempt to frame some of those questions.

Chapter 1

Towards an Interpretative Framework

In the past decade urban sociology has undergone a considerable change. Like its counterpart, urban geography, and like many other areas of sociology, it has been swept by a wave of Marxist writing. The origins of the 'new' urban sociology are found chiefly in the work of French scholars or of those who form part of a French 'school'. Thus, Lefebvre, Castells, Lojkine are most commonly identified as the founders of the new approach, but informing much of the debate and criticism – and underlying the work of those who follow Castells – the influence of Louis Althusser has been considerable.[1] Themes and issues developed in France or Italy have been seized with enthusiasm by a new generation of researchers in Britain and later the USA, and interwoven with diverse indigenous strands of leftist work to provide a broad range of frameworks and perspectives all claiming Marx and Engels as their source. The most generally influential ideas are rooted in Althusser's 'structural' interpretation of Marxist thought and these, together with insights provided by Gramsci or Lukács or others have come to constitute something approaching a new orthodoxy in the field, setting the agenda for debate and providing the lexicon for the new discourse.

The promise of Marxian approaches

The impact of the new ideas has been substantial. The 1970s saw much vigorous debate about the direction of urban research, new themes for investigation were identified and a general re-orientation called for.[2] Traditional urban sociology came under vigorous attack. At the broadest level, along with work in the rest of the social sciences, it was accused by Marxist scholars of showing too little concern for 'theory' – indeed, of totally misunderstanding the nature of 'theory'.

Thus, Castells[3] in his well-known article used the tools provided by Althusser to argue that bourgeois urban sociology provided no real theory but only ideology. Reviewing studies in the USA, Britain, France and elsewhere, he castigated researchers for their narrow empiricism, for their uncritical approach – their apparent willingness to serve the interests of planners, politicians and the more diffuse objectives of the capitalist system – and for failing to relate their concerns to what, in his view, constituted truly 'scientific' study. Under the influence of the preoccupations of American social science, urban sociology, he proclaimed, had become 'an ideology of modernity ethnocentrically identified with the crystallization of the social forms of liberal capitalism'.[4] Thus, in addressing themselves to the problems of integration and acculturation or in exploring patterns of residential segregation, or in compiling ethnographies of the diverse ethnic groups in the city, it was alleged, urban sociologists – especially American urban sociologists – had largely accepted the social and economic order in which they and their subjects were set. They had taken for granted, or so it was said, the dominant ideas and the formulations of 'problems' by the most powerful groups in contemporary western societies. By contrast, a Marxian standpoint conferred a distinctive, critical theory of knowledge and an approach which, based on an analysis of material – that is to say, economic – forces, afforded a distinctive angle of vision.

Such a claim did not originate with Castells but derived principally from the doyen of 'structural' Marxism, Louis Althusser. It was Althusser's conception of an alternative and superior epistemology which underpinned this attack and it was the 'structural' variant of Marxism which was greeted with applause by many researchers in urban sociology and urban geography[5] in recent years. It is important to recognize that within Marxist writings there exist different traditions, for as we shall see, they contribute different strengths and different weaknesses to the contemporary urban analysis, but certain general themes recur in most forms of recent Marxist work on cities and urban life.

Thus, it is argued, to understand the city – its physical and social development – we need to adopt an altogether wider perspective than that afforded by most 'bourgeois' sociology. We need to locate the city in an analysis of whole economic systems. Whether our focus is on the medieval city, on the industrial centres of nineteenth-century Britain or on urban settlements in today's third world, we need to begin from a conception of broad phases of capitalist development and the part played by cities in this.[6] The crowding, disease and squalor of British Victorian cities with their stark contrasts of wealth and poverty, their accommodation of much noxious, noisy industry right in their hearts can only be fully understood by recognizing the part played by urban growth in the early phases of industrial capitalism. The slums and shanty towns of Latin American cities must be seen as the products of successive periods of economic dependency on European and latterly North American capitalism.[7] And today, in Britain, the sprawling suburban settlements, the barrack-like ranks of public housing, the physical domination of the city centres by glass and steel office towers – all these must be apprehended as manifestations of an advanced or monopolistic stage of capitalistic growth.

We are invited then to use the tools of historical materialism to make sense of broad phases of urban development and also the precise character of social and political relationships within towns and between town and state. Central to such a perspective is the notion of class struggle. It is this which provides the dynamic in human affairs, carrying the development of society from one stage to the next and serving to structure the broadest range of social relations and social institutions. The force of much recent Marxist writing is to claim that in urban sociology the idea of class struggle has been grossly neglected. It is a claim with much substance to it. From the earliest work of the Chicago school to the texts and readers in urban sociology of the 1960s and 1970s, it is apparent that concern with class interests and class struggles has been minimal. But in the 'new' urban sociology all that is to change. Marxist writers will show us just how many of the urban institutions and practices we take for granted are really the product of class struggle. Thus, the provision of public housing for workers, the provision of schooling, the machinery of urban planning – all these can be seen as responses by dominant bourgeois groups to national and local class conflicts. In the interests of stability, the development of capitalism and their own protection, the bourgeois utilize the state and the local authorities to damp down class conflicts, often to anticipate class antagonism and ensure the reproduction of the existing systems of production and the labour force necessary for this working:

> Limited in Marx's time to the problems of housing and nourishment, the reproduction of labour power refers nowadays to

a complex set of collective means of consumption and an environment which are the historical product of class struggles.[8]

In most of the recent analyses, the conception of the class struggle retains its traditional Marxian character. Although white-collar workers, petit-bourgeois elements and professional groups receive occasional mention, the underlying notion is of conflict betwen two old antagonists: the proletariat and the bourgeoisie.

Concern with how the bourgeoisie maintains its power has led Castells and many other modern Marxists to a renewed interest in the role of the state and in particular to the provision by central and municipal authorities of 'collective' goods. According to Castells, urban issues are frequently at the heart of current political debates (his evidence, in fact, comes largely from France and Italy)[9] and this reflects the growing importance of what he calls 'collective consumption' in the lives of citizens of modern states.[10] Today the pervasiveness of public intervention in the planning and regulating of the environment, the scale of provision of roads, water supplies, recreational facilities, educational and medical services, and, above all, housing, means that conflicts revolve not only around workplace issues, but increasingly centre on the 'consumption' of collective goods. And, since many of these goods are created and distributed on a local basis, the urban and regional institutions are the locus of much 'political' action by groups seeking to influence their allocation. In recent Marxian writing, questions are raised as to how, precisely, we should conceive the relationship between the central state and the local authority, or the state, the municipalities and the bourgeoisie. There is room here for a good deal of argument – not only between Marxists and theorists of different persuasions – but also among Marxists themselves.[11] There are many who would take issue with, for instance, Cynthia Cockburn's[12] portrayal of the relationship between the state and the local authority but there is no denying that in a society like Britain, where social democratic policies have led to the provision of many public resources, that relationship, hitherto confined to one of the dustier corners of political science, deserves our attention.

The provision of collective goods by the state and its agencies creates the prospect of new inequalities and new struggles. It is obvious that in any allocative system there will be some who do less well than others. Britain's public housing system, for instance, operates with diverse local criteria of eligibility which serve to exclude or severely limit the access of some social categories: the young, the mobile or the immigrants. The stock of such housing also displays considerable variation in quality, from the relatively luxurious apartments or houses in highly desirable sites to crumbling tenements in the heart of the old industrial quarters of the inner city. And it is much the same with resources for health care or for education: the quality of provision is by no means even. For some Marxist writers, these disparities appear as likely sources of discontent and potential mobilization. Groups of neighbours, loose affiliations of tenants, and residents' associations have been portrayed, by Castells, Olives and others as 'urban social movements', whose presence creates the possibility of broadly based alliances, and of political action against the state or the city authorities which will unite citizens of different classes.[13] Given leadership and organisation, Castells sees these popular mobilizations as part of a new urban politics where the conflicts revolve less around the old social divisions of the productive system and more around the issues of 'collective consumption'. British and American writers have frequently expressed reservations both about the theoretical adequacy of the 'urban social movements' idea and about the likelihood of large-scale, cross-class and radical protest in the cities of Britain or North America. Pahl sees local protests over public resources as more likely to lead to fragmentation of existing class solidarities than to inter-class affiliations and S. M. Miller is doubtful about the chance of any 'new' urban politics in the USA.[14] None the less, the Marxian focus upon collective goods and collective action related to them has had the salutary effect of encouraging research on a wide variety of local protests and spontaneous action outside the framework of conventional political parties.[15] It seems generally true that more and more political action revolves around environment, housing and other 'consumption' matters and this makes the sporadic mobilizations of citizens fighting to preserve, protect or enhance their neighbourhoods and homes a matter of more than passing interest.

The impact of Marxism on urban sociology has been considerable. Even from this brief sketch it should be possible to understand the attractiveness of the apparently novel and radical approaches it commends. Marxism offers an encompassing and critical view of the development of western society and specifies important problems for theory and for practice. Its 'holism' gives it an aesthetic appeal and its certainties provide comfort from the ambiguities and confusions of so-called bourgeois studies. Small wonder then that so many social scientists have been won over, 'converted' by the resurgence of Marxist scholarships in recent years. The field of urban studies contains one of the most honest and explicit accounts of just such a 'conversion' in David Harvey's celebrated *Social Justice and the City*.[16] In the early chapters he writes as a 'liberal'; in the latter ones his whole approach is transformed as he struggles towards a materialist understanding of the urban processes he describes. Marxists then invite us to construct a 'political economy' of the city, to relocate our interests in urban growth or decline in urban social and physical structures, within a broader, societal view of economic change. They want us to see the city not as something special or set apart, but as the very product of general economic forces, of sweeping, historical changes and continuously evolving class struggles. They have identified a number of important researchable themes and within the field of study have pressed these to the centre of the stage, given them coherence and ensured that by contrast, many of the old ecological or ethnographic interests appear almost trivial.

The weaknesses of Marxian approaches

In urban studies, then, as elsewhere in sociology, we owe much to the stimulating and provocative essays of those who embrace Marxism. And yet there *are* some major obstacles to our acceptance of it as the definitive framework for our analysis. It is not our intention to construct a detailed and extensive critique of neo-Marxism in urban sociology and certainly not to mount any sort of gladiatorial display between 'Marxists' and 'Weberians'. However, we did embark on this book becase we felt considerable dissatisfaction with aspects of contemporary Marxism in this area and because we felt that some valuable insights, specific concepts and perspectives derived from Weber were being ignored or summarily dismissed. In the interests of brevity, we can focus our criticisms and misgivings on four aspects of contemporary Marxism:

1. The structuralist insistence on the primacy of 'theory' – holistic, materialist theory.
2. The rejection of history.
3. The portrayal of man as a mere agent of supra-human forces.
4. The treatment of class conflict.

The enthusiasm for 'theory' – grand, encompassing theory – owes most to Althusser's reworking of Marx and to his attempt to establish a distinctive and superior epistemology. By contrast with the attempts to construct limited, partial theories of particular social phenomena, found in most conventional 'bourgeois' sociology, structural Marxism insists on the necessity of seeing society 'as a whole' and constructing a holistic grand theory within which all human activity can be explained. Existing 'knowledge' found within the fragmented social science disciplines is dismissed not simply as partial, but ideological since the 'facts' with which they work arrive as it were pre-packaged, shaped and selected by political and theoretical predelictions which are 'incorrect' in so far as they do not proceed from a materialist conception of the social order. Thus, the first and most important task, according to this view, is to develop a comprehensive theory so that it can be seen that societies are more than the sum of their parts, so that it can be demonstrated that the whole determines the nature of the constituent elements whose character cannot be understood if studied in isolation or without recognition of their interrelatedness.

But how is this to be done? Other attempts to construct 'grand theories' in sociology or anthropology – Parsonian functionalism in sociology or structural functionalism in British anthropology or cultural anthropology in America – all have come in for a great deal of criticism and their proponents have, to a large extent, retreated to work in more modest ways on theories of the 'middle ground'.[17] Here it is to be done by recognizing the essential truth of Marx's words – and silences – as interpreted by Althusser. We are in the presence of a breathtaking, intellectual imperialism as distasteful to Marxists raised on a more modest, more humane tradition as to their bourgeois colleagues. E. P. Thompson's selection of a passage from Althusser's *Lenin and Philosophy*[18] makes this plain:

> the specialists who work in the domains of the 'Human Sciences' and of the Social Sciences (a smaller domain) i.e. economists, historians, sociologists, social psychologists, historians of art and literature, or religious and other ideologies – and even linguists and psychoanalysts, all these specialists ought to know that they cannot produce truly scientific knowledges in their specializations unless they recognise the indispensability of the theory Marx founded. For it is, in principle, the theory which 'opens up' to scientific knowledge

the 'continent' in which they work, in which they have so far only produced a few preliminary knowledges (linguistics, psychoanalysis) or a few elements or rudiments of knowledge (the occasional chapter of history, sociology, or economics) or illusions pure and simple, illegitimately called knowledges.

Neither Althusser nor any of his many followers have successfully *demonstrated* the superiority of structural Marxist theory. The whole thing rests upon an act of faith, a 'wager on the outcome of history'.[19] What they have constructed is a 'theology'. The new Marxism is no less 'ideological' than the forms of knowledge it seeks to displace. Moreover, though it claims to offer materialist explanations, in practice it serves up such abstracted accounts of structural relationships that it opens itself to the charge that what it really provides is a theoretical system as replete with 'idealism' as the systems it claims to despise.[20] The only difference is that it is now a Marxian 'idea' that suffuses the theory. Peter Worsley, commenting on the resurgence of western Marxism – and he is by no means unsympathetic to many aspects of that approach – has argued that the predeliction for dealing with the 'societal whole' has led to an 'over-socialization' of theory and that there seems to be 'absence of anything like an adequate conceptualization of levels of mediation, secondary association, etc., between "the society" and the local situation'.[21]

Such a deficiency seems common in many recent Marxist works in urban sociology. It is certainly a failing in Castells's *The Urban Question*. The task of good urban sociology must surely be to move from the grand design, the conception of the broad lineaments of social structure to the detailed and precise study of local social systems, local patterns of social relations and configurations of social collectivities. In their determination to steer our interests away from the small scale, the particular, many contemporary Marxian pieces seem to have embraced 'theory' rather too readily and somewhat prematurely – as Philip Abrams has suggested.[22]

Marxists can take much credit for opening up debate in the last decade, forcing us to think critically about the work that has been done in urban studies, but the time is surely ripe for variants of Marxism themselves to be appraised cooly. Peter Saunders seems to have caught the present mood and expresses a viewpoint with which we have much sympathy when he writes:

no single body of theory and no one paradigm can be expected to provide all the answers to the questions currently being posed in urban sociology . . . a degree of theoretical pluralism and epistemological tolerance is . . . an essential precondition for the future development of the discipline.[23]

The epistemological concerns of structural Marxism have led to another tendency in some recent work which we find objectionable. This is the rejection of history. History, as we saw in the quotation taken from Althusser, was one of those human sciences which had failed to recognize the supremacy of Marxist theory and which, in consequence, had allowed 'ideology' to pass as theory. The facts assembled and interrogated by historians were not 'real' objects of study. Even Marxist historians, according to this view, had failed to recognize that their 'knowledge' was based on nothing more than 'empiricism'; they had not noticed, in Thompson's words, that 'the attainment of historical knowledge has been misbegotten from the start'. As a historian who had long thought that his contribution to historical materialism *had* constituted genuine knowledge, Thompson is understandably upset to find that his labours, along with those of non-Marxist students of history are dismissed so lightly. He points, entirely justifiably, to the gross confusion which runs through the structuralist critique of 'empirical procedures, empirical controls' and something which he (Althusser) calls 'empiricism'.[24] And from Hindess and Hirst he takes a passage which provides the baldest statement of the rejection of history:

Marxism as a theoretical and a political practice, gains nothing from its association with historical writing and historical research. The study of history is not only scientifically but also politically valueless.[25]

To the extent that structural Marxism has gained a hold on urban sociology, it has served to steer debate and research away from historical themes. It helps to explain why relatively few urban sociology projects have much of an historical dimension and this seems especially lamentable when we consider that the study of urban history has made such strides in recent years.[26] Work in urban sociology which does have an historical dimension for the most part remains non-Marxian in character, or draws – and this seems increasingly common – on other non-structuralist traditions.[27] The rekindling of interest in Marxism which began a decade or so ago appeared to hold the promise of a more historically informed sociology. Philip Abrams, in his 1972 inaugural lecture, having made approving reference to structuralism, to Piaget and to Althusser, observed: 'So far as I can see Marx provides us with the only substantially developed model we have of what a historical sociology would be.'[28] And he went on:

> Whether or not we are convinced by Marx's conclusions his method strikes me as entirely compelling . . . it is a method which makes its own conclusions available for empirical evaluation — it grounds its theory of transition in the study of concrete historical experience and relationships.

Sadly, in urban sociology the promise remains largely unfulfilled. The concern with 'theory', the suspicion with which the empirical mode of investigation has been viewed have dissipated and diverted much of the effort.

The third of our misgivings has to do with the treatment of class and class conflict in structural Marxism. As Foster[29] observes, in Castells's work, class struggle is treated in an abstracted, formal way. The emphasis on the overall system and the conviction that 'explanation' of class conflict can be reached only at the level of the most general 'contradictions' leads to grossly inadequate discussion of social consciousness. It is true that class tensions have their origins in the economic structures of the society as a whole, or indeed, in the capitalist system as a whole, but actual mobilizations of poeple, particular forms of protest, are rooted in historically and locationally specific situations:

> to deal with real people caught and held in particular historical circumstances, we need a degree of definition about *how* existing levels of popular culture and organisation enclose the gains of past struggle.[30]

We need to know about the actual conditions of labour, the details of particular systems of production and consumption, the diverse cultural and ideological traditions, the forms of working-class leadership and political organisation in particular towns and regions, if we are to make sense of class consciousness and class action. The work by Castells and his colleagues and followers on 'urban social movements' rarely attends to these matters in anything like the detail thought appropriate by more orthodox Marxists or by many bougeois historians and sociologists.[31]

Thus, though we have been instructed by Althusser that 'class struggle is the motor of history', most of the urban work which hangs upon his theoretical elaboration leaves us profoundly ignorant of the realities of class *experience*, of class relations as they are lived. As E. P. Thompson has told us many times:

> Class does not precede but arises out of struggle . . . classes arise because men and women in determinate productive relations, identify their antagonistic interests and come to struggle, to think, and to value in class ways; thus, the process of class formation is a process of self-making.[32]

Such a view is a long way from the 'mechanical', system-directed, system-given conceptualizations of the Althusserians.

There is too, in structuralist urban sociology, a resolute determination to sustain, in its imagery of the contemporary cities, that 'procrustean dualism,[33] which Marx claimed to observe in mid-nineteenth-century Britain. The battle lines are clearly drawn: here the bourgeoisie, there the proletariat. But surely we should ask whether such a simple representation is adequate for our analysis of the complex social and economic relations of today's world. Much of the persuasiveness of the original argument rested on the plausibility of a dichotomic representation of the social structure, with the privileged class of property owners confronted by an impoverished, exploited and, so it appeared, increasingly solidary working class. However, the gap between theory and observable reality has widened to the point where attempts to press the diversities of contemporary social structure into the old mould stretch our credibility. How should we locate the numerous white-collar workers, the technical experts, managers, teachers and administrators? Can we accept, as Castells does, the classifications offered by Poulantzas[34] whereby the proletariat is reduced to a rump of manual workers performing 'productive' labour – that is, labour which contributes to surplus value without being involved in any supervisory role – and an enormous class, the 'new petty bourgeoisie', which comprises technicians, foremen, managers, public adminstrative employees and teachers bound together by their ideological disposition (rather than their structural location) and linked thereby to the classical bourgeoisie?[35] We think not.

The real complexity and untidiness of class conflicts in particular cities, and the sharpness of many confrontations, is often lost in over-arching arguments of many contemporary works in urban sociology. There is a noticeable coyness about discussing *intra*-class conflicts. But the fact is that now, as ever, those workers who are highly skilled or highly organized or in a location which gives them a measure of coercive power, do not necessarily identify with the lot of the unskilled or the unorganized. Different positions in the systems of production, differential access to resources like housing, schools and other publicly provided goods often divide the working class. And these internal differences among workers have their counterparts among white-collar, professional, managerial or entrepreneurial groups. In the histories of our cities, these intra-class conflicts have very real consequences, affecting the character of local political elites, the social and economic policies and opportunities in the area and a wider perspective can be seen to reflect or influence the fortunes of nationally defined strata and classes.

Though class interests provide the most general, indeed, the indispensable basis for the analysis of social conflict in the city, they do not capture the full range of social divisions. Take, for instance, the matter of race or ethnicity. Whether we look at American cities with their black ghettos or at the racial or cultural divisions of Canadian urban areas (the segregation of Anglophones and Francophones in Montreal, the history of discriminatory legislation against the Chinese in Vancouver or Victoria) or at the recent ugliness of racial confrontations in British cities, it is plain that ethnic as well as class divisions must find a place in our analysis. While we may point to certain objective similarities in the class positions of black and white workers or to the similarity of their long-term goals, the fact is that racial and ethnic differences matter: they matter in terms of the consciousness of immigrant and indigenous populations, they matter as sources of individual identity and of communal sensibility. They fracture the organisations of the working class, impinge on political life and give rise to spatially distinct areas of our cities. We may lament this. But we cannot ignore it.

Ethnic divisions are essentially *status* divisions, and status as an analytically distinct dimension of power is not be be dismissed lightly if we really wish to understand the social and economic life of cities. In so far as class interests extend beyond the confines of the locality and provide the bases for some sense of identity with a nation-wide 'working class' or 'middle class' and in so far as class interests are proclaimed and defended in the realm of national politics, the local arena becomes one in which people can attend more closely to their status concerns. They can, and do, seek to protect their neighbourhoods, pubs, schools and other elements of their 'ways of life', or to promote their particular group and its affiliates. That may mean trying to win political control, trying to monopolize economic opportunities or simply claiming deference from 'inferior' social categories. Frequently it involves all these, as the voluminous community studies literature testifies. In the attack on 'bourgeois' urban sociology, the continuing significance of status groups and status-based conflicts in the cities has been submerged.

So too, religious divisions receive scant attention, yet historically these have been of great moment, playing directly into the political arena as candidates stood and parties were formed to represent distinctive ideals. Areas became predominantly Catholic or resolutely Protestant, as in Glasgow or Liverpool or many urban centres in the USA. Fundamentalist sects imposed their ideas on the institutions and ways of life of districts in the city, banning pubs or dance halls or other iniquitous places of entertainment. Even within a Protestant variant, like Presbyterianism, divisions occurred – as between adherents of the Church of Scotland and those professing the more austere faith of the 'Free Kirk' – with considerable impact on the social and political life of a city like Aberdeen.[36] Nor is it all 'mere history'. One need only think about the ecological segregation,[37] the gerrymandering of constituencies and wards, the allocation of jobs and houses[38] – the whole bitter legacy of sectarianism in Belfast or Londonderry – to see the point.

Thus, though we would agree with Marxists that we must always start with the analysis of material interests and of the class locations of groups in the city, it is essential that we explore in some detail the internal divisions of classes and the alternative, status bases for social organisation and social action. So far historians have given us much fuller accounts of such complex structures than have sociologists.

Finally, we can turn to the most general of our misgivings about the structuralist strand in recent urban work: its portrayal of man as a mere 'agent' of the all-important 'structures'. Althusser insists that we must focus, must take as our subjects, not 'real' men but the *places* occupied and the *functions* performed and the ways in which these are shaped by the relations of production. Castells shares this view as we can see in his discussions of how we should set about analysing social structures. He presents us with a choice:

> The theoretical issue is this: historical actors founding society through their action, or support-agents expressing combinations of social structure through their practice. We will take for granted . . . that only the second is capable of founding a science of society.[39]

So, much of the new urban sociology portrays man as a creature whose actions are, in the final analysis, *determined* by the systems in which he is set. We are a long way from the interests of Marx, especially evident in his earlier work, in human agency, in the human capacities and potentialities for changing the world. Much neo-Marxism leads us towards a form of social system analysis which, with its emphasis on 'locations' and 'functions' and the disembodied structure of structures, reminds us of the more grandiose schemes of the functionalists, and like that mode of analysis, is open (despite its avowed 'radicalism') to charges of conservatism and stasis.

Again, as in earlier grand theories, neo-Marxian writing shows a disturbing proclivity for reification. The key elements in the structural analysis begin to take on a life of their own and are invested with capacities stolen from 'concrete individuals' or groups of actors. Thus, Capital acts, Capital seeks to intervene, contradictions act and press, we have interventions by the institutional system as a whole and plenty about Capitalism's logic.[40] The use of such phrases amounts to much more than a stylistic device. It accurately conveys a conception of society and man in which the latter is stripped of his ideas and ideals, deprived of his culture and history and his capacity to act, to struggle, to resist. He is an actor for whom the script is written and the director (Capitalism) allows little improvisation.

There is in all this a conspicuous failure to explore what Thompson calls the 'dialogue' between social being and social consciousness,[41] a failure to examine how men make sense of their lives, how they live the experience of dominance or repression, how they interpret their positions and with these interpretations fabricate institutions, organisations and ideals – both defensive and subversive.

Much of the neo-Marxist writing then seems to us to have constructed an 'inauthentic model of man'.[42] In urban sociology, no less than in urban geography there is the need for a more humanistic approach, one which does not dispense with the idea of structure but which returns the problems of 'meaning' and 'action' to the centre of our analysis. What we are commending is a social action approach which sees society

> not as a supra-human, self-generating, and self-maintaining entity, but as a humanly accomplished social world, a social system conceptualized as the emergent product of the social action and interaction of members.[43]

General features of an interpretative framework

Our task then is to outline an approach which is not 'anti-Marxist' but which is sceptical of some of the more grandiose and dogmatic claims made in its name and specifically to reject the mechanical and reductionist view of man as the mere expression of material forces. We wish to point students to analyses and concepts derived principally from the work of Max Weber which seem to offer a return to a more interpretative approach to human society and to the study of the city. We do so because the current enthusiasm for material explanations leaves unused many valuable concepts found in the theoretical lockers of the discipline. And, also, because the particular variants of Marxism which have recently appeared in urban sociology seem so often to lead us away from those presentations, found in older forms of Marxism as well as in 'bourgeois' sociology, which invite us to explore the consciousness of men and which give their thoughts and motives an important place in our quest for understanding. Turning to Weber rather than to Marx, we shall not try to raise an 'idealist' banner in opposition to a 'materialist' one, indeed if we want to find 'idealism' we need look no further than structural Marxism itself. The task is to encourage appreciation *both* of the realities of material life – the real differences of experience and interest of different groups and classes – *and* the constellations of ideas and sentiments with which men make sense of their lives. As Dawe says of a social action approach, it is not a perspective which

> denies the manifest existence of constraint. Rather it locates

constraint not in an entity external to and superordinate over man, but quite simply in the action of other actors; that is, in humanly constructed structures of power and domination. To paraphrase Sartre, constraint is other people.[44]

There is nothing especially novel in what we are recommending. In other areas of sociology, in the study of class and stratification, for instance, such an approach can be found in the work of writers like Lockwood, Goldthorpe, Giddens, Mann, Bell, Newby and many others. Marxist students like to refer to it as 'left-Weberianism'. So be it. The adjective signals the fact that we need not take on board all Weber's personal political views when we approve his general approach or utilize a number of his concepts.

What are the hallmarks of this orientation? First, it is one which sees human relations as essentially and irrevocably conflictual and human societies and communities as collectivities structured by those conflicts. Group conflict – and it is that rather than individual conflict that interests us – is a normal, not a pathological condition. Groups and their conflictual relations one to another are very much at the heart of Weber's work and the view he takes of the human condition is one of the points of agreement between his analysis and that of Marx. Both these classic writers begin with an interest in the problem of how men can regain control over their own affairs.

> The solution lies in the unceasing attempt to exert human control through social action over existing institutions, relationships, situations and systems in such a way as to bring them into line with human construction of their ideal meaning.[45]

But whereas Marx came to a vision of some resolution of this state of affairs, Weber foresaw no ultimate revolution which could settle basic social oppositions. It is not necessary to view endemic conflict as something to be lamented; rather, it is to be looked upon as the source of stimulation, innovation and change. Thus, in the city, while not ignoring those things making for cohesion, harmony, or consensus, we shall focus upon the structuring of conflict: the ways in which different social groups have struggled for control of the city, how status groups and ethnic groups as well as classes, have sought to gain and maintain economic and social and political power in the urban centres.

Second, our treatment of urban society will stress complexity and contingency in human affairs. We can portray actors as located in analytically separable structures – political, social and economic – with their constituent arrays of institutions and associations and patterns of social relationships. We can point to the coexistence of diverse systems of ideas and values and the contiguity of varied types of social action and in this way hope to represent something of the real ambiguity that characterizes human action. A Weberian approach cannot offer such confident generalisations as distinguish much of the neo-Marxian writing, rather it must rejoice in the indeterminacy, the incompleteness, the contingency which informs social arrangements and facilitates the survival, side by side, of diverse social groupings, systems of ideas and economic structures. Thus, though we may seek some general features of 'medieval' or 'early modern' or 'industrial' cities, we should strive to retain an awareness of the rich variety of political and economic relations that are to be found in each of these.

Third , an analysis of urban centres, as of societies as a whole, must be historically rooted. Here too there is a substantial agreement with pre-Althusserian Marxism, but Weber's extensive comparative studies of societies and periods other than his own, did not lead to a 'directional' view of history. He explored the divergent paths of economic development taken by various social orders and if we were to follow his 'model' of scholarship, we should place more value on detailed studies of historical developments in particular towns and show less enthusiasm for argument about 'stages' and 'phases' of economic development. Following the Weber model in urban studies would seem a highly desirable thing to do in sociology at the present time, for we cannot really make sense of recent struggles in our urban centres without much better historical information. The study of how our cities, say, in Britain, have acquired their particular physical, economic and social patternings, the precise ways in which class interests or the ambitions of distinct status groups or economic institutions shaped them, is still in its infancy. A few painstaking reconstructions of recent urban developments, from the Victorian period to the present day, are being undertaken by sociologists (and we owe a considerable debt to some of the Community Development Projects in this regard), but generally our urban sociology has a poor appreciation of historical process.[46] Yet such work is essential not only for our knowledge of the broad structures of power but for the material out of which to construct those connections between 'biography and history' which are prerequisites for an interpretation of social action.

Following Weber, we should be curious about the diverse forms of associational life in the city and the ways in which these have changed as urban centres have grown and been encapsulated within the modern state and modern economies. Oath-bound fraternities of burghers have disappeared, as have guilds and many other corporate bodies but in the transition from medieval to modern cities, other modes of collective action have developed. One way of looking at this is to consider how forms of contentious or defiant behaviour have developed.[47] Cities have always been remarkable for the extent of their internal differentiation – differentiation by trade, religion, ethnicity or neighbourhood – and as the bases for social differentiation have altered, so too have the means by which men and women express their discontent and struggle for power and for justice. The use of ritualized mockery, of street theatre seen on market or feast days or other public holidays in seventeenth- and eighteenth-century cities gave way in the nineteenth century to organized demonstrations, strikes and protest orchestrated by formally constituted, special interest associations. Forms of collective action become institutionalized, come to constitute more or less clearly recognized 'repertoires' of public behaviour. Today, though we continue to use many of the devices created in the course of the last century, new forms of collective action, new forms of associational life are emerging, reflecting the changing character of our economies and polities. As forms of domination have changed so too have the collective responses. Today there are discernible new forms of protest frequently organized around conflicts over public property, seeking ways around the rigidities of the party system and the approved modes of representation, seeking too to challenge the impositions of bureaucratic authority.

Fourth, we need a 'political economy' of the city which assigns the specifically 'political' dimension more importance, more autonomy. A 'political economy' approach which owed a little more to Weber and a little less to Marx would see politics as much more than a reflection of class interests and class struggles. Martin Spencer, in his article on *The City*, describes Weber's portrayal of the relationship between economics and politics:

Economic development does not proceed in the fashion of a

progressive unfolding of the potential of given institutional arrangements that then generate new forces destined to become the 'negation' of the first. We have rather a complex of economic systems and activities represented by groups that stand in a favoured relationship to those activities. the direction of economic development is determined by the political triumph of one or another groups. There is nothing predetermined or inevitable about the result.[48]

This does not deny the importance of 'material bases'. Weber is quite clear about the fact that political control commonly falls into the hands of economically powerful groups but he asserts the complexity of political struggles and the politically contingent character of economic development. In particular cities, now as in the medieval city-states, we find various groups forming themselves into parties and contending for control of our cities. In Britain there are the local representatives of national parties – Labour, Conservative, Liberal – but there are also non-aligned associations representing ratepayers, reform movements and a host of other interests. There are class-based parties and others based on status, ethnicity or language. The outcomes of the struggles really do matter in terms of the economic, and other policies that are pursued. Cities like Edinburgh and Glasgow, a mere forty miles apart, have had very different political histories and the groups which have held power not only reflect the quite different economic bases of the two urban economies, but also the struggle between status groups and the formulation of distinct ideologies which have informed the economic and social policies which (especially over the past half century or so) have done so much to accentuate their remarkable divergences.

The histories of these two centres makes it very plain that cities can enjoy marked changes in their fortunes and in their relative standing within nation-wide systems of cities. Cities grow, but they also decline, and not just in terms of population but also in terms of their cultural importance and the economic power which is concentrated in them. Glasgow was once Britain's second city, but no one would describe it that way today. Montreal was once the commercial centre of Canada, but from the 1960s onward Toronto challenged that supremacy and in recent years has overtaken its sister in Quebec. Who can deny that *political* considerations – latterly the rise of French Canadian nationalism – have contributed substantially to that change?[49] So far, sociologists in Britain have shown little interest in the decline of cities (unlike their colleagues in history who have a wider view of these things), yet that is an issue which makes very clear the contingent nature of urban life and demands careful, detailed and comparative study of *political* as well as economic factors for its full appreciation.

Finally, in this catalogue of general exhortations, we would argue that by taking Weber seriously we can go some way towards 'bringing' the people back in. As every first-year student learns, Weber's sociology is *'verstehen sociologie'*, concerned above all with the interpretative *understanding* of the *subjective* bases for action. An adequate urban sociology must provide a way of treating people as sentient beings with complex, frequently incoherent, sometimes inconsistent, sets of attitudes, values and beliefs, beings whose actions require the use of our imaginations to grasp how their collective efforts may be shaped both by the contexts in which they are set and the content of their sentiments and ideas. Of course, the actions of broad groups and classes are moulded by material considerations, but never by these alone. An interpretative approach to the study of urban life and urban processes requires us to explore the ideas, systems of belief and condensatory symbols which make possible action on the basis of shared meanings.

So much for broad objectives. We need to move on to consider exactly which elements from Weber's work will give us good service, but before we do so, perhaps we should pause to answer a pertinent question. Why are we interested in the city as such? It can easily be objected that the age of the city is dead, that cities no longer enjoy the kind of autonomy that medieval urban settlements did or that in highly urbanized societies the contrasts between town and country have largely disappeared – the city is everywhere. It is true that in most parts of the world today the city is subordinate to the nation-state and true too that the influence of cities over their hinterlands grows ever more extensive. Even in a physical sense, the city has lost its integrity. Today with no walls to contain them, urban settlements spread and sprawl over vast areas, destroying the distinctions between urban institutions and national ones, and since we are enmeshed in a world system of economic and political relations, we may well have to go beyond the boundaries of the nation-state. But this does not mean that the city is no longer a proper object of study.

In the so-called developed world, the overwhelming proportion of the population lives in the cities. For most of us, the city and its suburbs provide the locus for most of our activities – our work, our leisure pursuits, our domestic lives – and though the state may make decisions that affect us profoundly, the effects frequently reach us through local agencies and local administrations. There may be attempts to create national housing policies, but our opportunities to own or rent will vary greatly from one urban area to another for housing is available through local markets or local systems of allocation. And so it is with leisure or cultural resources or job opportunities.

Now, as ever, cities and their suburbs can be viewed as massive concentrations of economic and political power wielded by private enterprises and by public authorities. Many of the resources which have the most fundamental bearing on our lives are controlled or influenced by urban political and economic systems. This is not to argue that cities are 'autonomous' – we need to beware the influence of that ideology of city autonomy proclaimed by many local politicians – but it is to claim that local markets and local firms matter and that local political or administrative agencies, though generally subservient to the state, are not without some independence. Throughout this book we shall try to sustain the idea that the city remains an important arena for social conflict even in a highly developed, highly centralized society like Britain. And Britain and British cities will be our primary focus.

But what, exactly, can we take from Weber to guide us in our analysis? First and foremost, we can draw upon his political sociology and though we may find much of value in his essay *'The City'*, we shall plainly have to go beyond this piece to round out his ideas about power and authority. We shall have to look too at his writing about social stratification, for, though his work on this was not completed, it affords a way of challenging and modifying Marxian views on the nature of social cleavages and the structuring of conflict. Weber's writing about 'class', 'status' and 'party', and later developments of his ideas by so-called neo-Weberians, have much to offer when we try to make sense of contemporary urban life. So too do his celebrated reflections on the nature and growth of bureaucracy and the emergence of a numerous and powerful stratum involved in the administration of industrial, commercial and governmental enterprises.

When you write about or observe human societies, it is difficult to avoid discussion of the fact that in almost all human groupings there are some who appear to exercise control and others who appear to be subordinate. Weber wrote extensively about these relationships of superiority and inferiority in what has come to be called his sociology of domination. In the passages where he discusses the matter most explicitly, Weber observes that domination can take many forms and be based on diverse sources of 'superiority'. We can talk of domination in an everyday sense – of husbands 'dominating wives' (or vice versa), of teachers 'dominating' their charges – but these common-sense usages are not what really concerns us. Weber distinguished two 'pure' forms of domination: domination through the monopoly of interests and domination through 'authority'. In a market society, we can use the idea of domination to refer to the monopolistic powers of individuals or corporations. Think about the power of the oil companies or industrial giants like ITT or General Motors, or better still for our purposes, think about the power of the corporation in single-industry towns. That kind of 'domination' is important, crucially important, in many of the more recently urbanized parts of the world[50] and generally much more obvious and significant now than in the period when Weber wrote. But this type of domination interested Weber less than the other kind: domination involving 'authority'. Domination of this latter kind involved two elements: the power to command and the duty to obey. Domination here involves *legitimation*. Those who obey do so because they have come to believe in the rightness, the appropriateness of obedience. They 'ought' to obey. It is as though they have accepted the values on which the order is based, the interests it serves, and taken these as their own.

It is the trick of all successful rulership to persuade others that their compliance springs freely from their own wishes, that is, expresses their own desires. It is a trick which can be worked in several ways, which is precisely what Weber explores. There is the authority of tradition that underwrites the directives of African kings, medieval European princes (and most of the sillier rules of colleges and universities). There is the personal authority of leaders held to possess special gifts or 'charisma' which we see when we study many social or religious movements and from time to time we can observe it in the sphere of politics *per se*. Charismatic authority confronts problems of succession; traditional authority is hard to sustain in social systems oriented to the future and organized on 'rational' grounds. Thus, the most familiar form of legitimation is the appeal to formal rules, to legal specification of eligibility for office, to the rights of office holders with relevant expertise. The authority of our political leaders, of civil servants, of office holders in business organisations, derives from the rational rules which determine the competences and spheres of influence of the incumbents. Authority in such systems is not personal but vested in the office.

Domination is never total (even with today's sophisticated techniques of repression, dissidence is always possible), rather it is partial and precarious. Authority can be challenged on many grounds: specific competences may be judged 'outmoded', the discharge of responsibilities held to be inadequate. Office holders may be alleged to have extended their influence 'illegitimately' or some of the privileges of office may come to be viewed as insupportable. Groups with new interests, new skills, new resources are constantly emerging and seeking to claim the positions of power for themselves. And what contributes to the precariousness of all forms of domination is the fact that relationships of superiority and subordination are multiple and complex, that legitimate authority in, let us say, the political sphere is 'cashed out' in terms of economic privileges and the trappings of high social status. Repudiation of legitimate authority can, and frequently does, begin by attacks on the perks and privileges and status appropriated by those in office. Our cities, now as in the past, provide marvellous laboratories in which to observe and analyse the changing forms of domination, the rise and fall of dynasties, status groups and classes.

Weber certainly saw cities in this light. He studied the medieval cities in order to see how subordinate groups toppled the diverse rulerships, how legitimate domination was supplanted by new 'non-legitimate' regimes. To talk about much of this, he used the term 'usurpation' to refer to the encroachment by subordinate groups on the privileges and resources of a dominant one. In medieval European cities, noble (or merely rich) families usurped the powers of princes and bishops. They took control of the markets, the systems of taxation, the appointment of magistrates, sometimes effecting this in a revolutionary way, at others, doing so by negotiation. And then, one way or another, they transformed what Spencer[51] calls 'informal' power into 'formal' power. In Weber's terminology 'power' turned into domination. It became legitimized. Charters were given and the patricians and their bourgeois allies set about consolidating their position, glossing over the illegitimate way they had acquired and exercised power and seeking and expanding their control over economic resources and all the trappings of superiority.

The idea of usurpation does more than encompass some arcane details of medieval urban history. It provides a link to Weber's writing on social stratification and proves serviceable in the analysis of struggles in the contemporary city. For Weber, to study social stratification was to study power, but whereas Marxian writing ultimately traces all power back to a material base and clings to dualism of 'propertied' and 'propertyless', his scheme asserts the multi-dimensional character of power. Societies, in his view, contain not only class divisions, hierarchies reflecting the different market situations of groups and individuals, but also cleavages based on social honour or on the extent and kind of political power. His 'class' dimension yields a theoretical infinity of classes – as many as there are distinguishable market situations – but in practice, four broad aggregations emerge. These he itemized as:

(a) Those 'occupying a privileged position through property or education'.
(b) The 'intelligentsia' – those whose social position is primarily dependent on technical training, such as engineers, commercial and other office holders and civil servants.
(c) The 'lower middle class' of independent producers, retailers and other small businessmen.
(d) The 'working class' of propertyless manual workers.[52]

Plainly, such a system relieves us of the responsibility, felt acutely by most Marxist writers, of having to accommodate the great diversity of non-manual workers in one or other of the 'bourgeois' or 'proletarian' categories. Weber, writing with the advantages of a good many years, saw, more clearly than Marx, the importance of the growing numbers of administrators, managers, teachers and others who trade on their qualifications. His less rigid definition of class also encourages examination of many of the struggles which take place within, as it were, the 'economic dimension' – struggles in which groups seek to usurp the privileges of their superiors: semi-skilled workers seeking to obtain the pay and security of skilled workers, white-collar groups like social workers claiming 'professional' status and thereby some of the autonomy and perks enjoyed by the long-established groups like doctors and lawyers. 'Intra-', as well as 'inter-'

class conflict becomes a matter of very considerable interest, as does the relationship between classes and status groups and parties.

Inside our cities today, we can observe status struggles taking place *within* broad class aggregations. In urban areas in Britain or the USA, in Germany, Holland and France, in Canada and Australia, the working class is riven by racial, religious and ethnic conflicts. White workers attempt to preserve their jobs, their political supremacy, their districts, their institutions from 'invasion' by non-whites; anglophones exclude francophones, Protestants debar Catholics from areas of housing and employment. Race, ethnicity, religion – all three constitute bases for the differential allocation of social honour, for relatively distinctive patterns of consumption or styles of life. And different status levels connote different chances in the hierarchy of class.

It was in his discussion of status groupings that Weber employed the notion of 'social closure' and recently this idea has been used by Frank Parkin in his attempt to find new ways of analysing the social divisions of contemporary western societies. 'Closure' refers to the processes 'by which social collectivities seek to maximise rewards by restricting access to resources and opportunities to a limited circle of eligibles'.[53] Dominant groups, whether at the level of the city or the wider society, generally try to monopolize specific opportunities, especially economic opportunities. Thus, we can observe the rules about 'whites only' jobs in South Africa, the practices of excluding blacks from colleges and workplaces and housing areas which have required legislation partially to offset them in the USA. We can read the unsavoury history of the exclusion of Chinese Canadians from jobs and from the electoral rolls of parts of Western Canada or uncover the political chicanery that kept Catholics out of well-paid jobs and in the ghettos of Northern Ireland's cities. These exclusionary practices constitute, in Parkin's view, a form of exploitation of the subordinate groups and in many instances, have been productive of what we might consider an alternative and complementary mode of 'closure'. Faced with institutionalized blockages to their social and political and economic ambitions, subordinate groups frequently come to recognize their state as one of 'exploitation' – a process which involves at least a partial rejection of the legitimating rhetorics – and they then react. They do so by striving to capture some of the economic, political or social privileges of superordinate groups. They try to usurp them.

Parkin is claiming that to grasp the character of major cleavages in contemporary societies, we should focus less on the 'attributes' of social aggregates: whether they occupy blue-collar or white-collar jobs, whether they possess capital of one or another kind or are propertyless. Instead we should look at the ways in which classes and strata seek to maintain or challenge privileges by what he calls 'contrary principles of social action'. In other words, by whether they engage primarily in 'exclusionary' action or 'usurpatory' action. Rising groups, rising classes act to displace the incumbents of positions of power. They are principally concerned to exert, through collective action, pressure in an upward direction in their efforts to resist exploitation and ultimately to gain access to resources and opportunities. Though they may simultaneously operate some mechanism of exclusion against social orders lower than themselves, they are generally more interested in acting in ways which broaden their boundaries, widen their bases and thus carry with them in the fight some whom they may latterly disown. This surely has been the pattern in many western cities when lower middle-class elements fought for representation and formed parties to win municipal elections. At first they were keen to represent their interests as essentially similar to those of the manual workers and they were vigorous in soliciting support from proletarian elements in their battles with the big bourgeois and established aristocratic power holders. But once they achieved a dominant position in the local hierarchies of the town hall, they began to formulate protective, exclusionary plans and those whom they excluded were their erstwhile allies in the working class.

Our own research on the history of Edinburgh's municipal affairs will allow us to document quite clearly the changing strategies of an intermediate stratum of petit-bourgeois characters seeking and winning control over city affairs. And today, in many places, it is possible to watch an increasingly numerous bureaucratic stratum acting in some rather similar ways as it seeks representation of its interests and in some instances, local domination in the name of what is sometimes talked of as a 'new class'. Our consideration of the growth of what Weber categorized as an 'intelligentsia' at a national level and its rapid expansion within local government bureaucracies will allow us to explore this theme further.

The idea of 'social closure' will help us to interpret many of the forms of collective action which can be observed in urban areas. The quest for domination, the attempt at defence and protection against exploitation, serves to give some broad structure to social relations at a local level. It is out of this attempt at closure that those bonds and alliances we take as constituting 'community' arise. Those groups which succeed in establishing a high degree of closure are more likely to be successful in their usurpatory struggles and the bonds of community between them, once they have established themselves as a dominant group, can then be refined and strengthened through exclusionary devices: identifying groups of inferiors and using a series of symbols to label them and keep them in subordination. These processes are surely observable whether we are looking at the domination of WASP elements in US cities and the stigmatisation and exclusion of blacks and Puerto Ricans and others, or at the formation of those urban fraternities of noble families that established themselves as the masters of the artisan and petit-bourgeois and non-Christian elements in a medieval city.

These then are some of the broad themes, some of the general concepts which we can employ in an attempt to sketch a neo-Weberian, social action approach to the study of the city. Let us begin with Weber's only sustained commentary on the city. Let us begin with history.

Chapter 2

The Medieval Cities: The Struggles for Domination

Introduction

Max Weber's essay 'The City' must rank as one of the best-known but least-read contributions to sociology; it is also one of the most selectively interpreted of his writings. Most students of urban sociology have heard about it, as have a good many following courses in urban geography, planning or politics and every year many of them read Don Martindale's famous introduction, but Weber's text itself usually defeats all but a few. And this is hardly surprising for it is a complex piece of work in which it is easy to lose sight of major arguments as they weave in and out of the author's classificatory schemes or as they vanish behind the framework of erudite historical detail from which the whole is constructed.

Many come to it expecting to find a general theory of 'the city', expecting to discover a distinctive account of urban settlements as special kinds of human grouping, expecting, in fact, that Weber like many other writers would be trying to show that the conditions of urban existence gave rise to rather special cultural and institutional responses on the part of those who live there. Martindale's prefatory comment with its discussion of the city 'as a distinctive form of human organisation' encourages this expectation, as does his endorsement of 'Louis Wirth's proposition that Weber's study is one of the closest approximations to a theory of urbanism that we have'.[1] Certainly it is possible to read the essay this way, but to do so is a mistake. We would agree with Philip Abrams's recent observation:

> It is an odd irony that although cities figure in Weber's own analysis only as legal and institutional expressions . . . of real and very concretely organised impositions or usurpations of power on the part of very clearly defined social groups, his discussion of these processes should have been commonly interpreted as though it was

a contribution to a theory of the city involving a peculiarly simple notion of the essence of urbanism as a matter of communal association. He has thus been treated as an arch perpetrator of an error . . . which he almost uniquely avoided making.[2]

Though Weber did explore the various definitions of cities which had been employed, and though he made some distinctions between types of cities – 'consumer' versus 'producer' cities or 'patrician' versus 'plebeian' – he was not seeking any universal characteristics from which, in the manner of some later sociologists, he could deduce patterned, recurrent social effects. What interested Weber most about the ancient and medieval cities were the opportunities they afforded for studying the operation of power in society. Cities were places to which men came in the hope of gaining power, but they were also centres of refuge *from* power. Some came with high hopes of economic success, or a specialist education or some political preferment. Others came in order to escape the exercise of feudal authority in the countryside; they came to be free. The cities of medieval Europe were especially interesting because they were the locus of many of the most fundamental changes in the transition from feudalism to modern society. Inside them it was possible to see how groups jockeyed for position, to explore the bases of their authority, to watch some expand their power and influence, and others mobilize to resist illegitimate demands and sometimes to contrive the overthrow of a dominant minority. It was possible to observe the historic struggles between different classes and status groups, the clashing of systems of ideas, the emergence of new institutions, the establishment of new forms of social relationship.

Weber then was not interested in the city *sui generis* as the fact that he so seldom refers to urbanisation or city life in the rest of his work makes plain. He was interested in power and social conflict and broad patterns of social change. And because it is these very broad themes which lie at the heart of his essay on the medieval and ancient cities, we can find there, beneath all the historiographic detail, a general perspective and some basic concepts which have considerable relevance and value in the study of the modern city.

Interpretations

Many of the well-known commentaries on Weber's sociology ignore

The City completely. Parsons, in *The Structure of Social Action*[3] makes no reference to it; Freund, *The Sociology of Max Weber*[4] and Eldridge in *Max Weber: the Interpretation of Social Reality*[5] make only a passing reference to it and Giddens in *Capitalism and Modern Social Theory*[6] has no discussion of the work. One of the few writers who finds the essay of interest is Bendix[7] and it is in his treatment of *The City* that we encounter the argument that it contains much that is central to Weber's major sociological concerns. Bendix's account tries to show how the analysis of medieval cities contributes to Weber's interest in the growth of economic rationality and the 'uniqueness of the west'. In doing so, he ties *The City* very closely to the famous essay on *The Protestant Ethic and the Spirit of Capitalism*.[8] He argues that the medieval European cities with their freedom and notion of citizenship, their distinctive laws and fostering of economic rationality, laid the foundations for the rise of capitalism and the seedbed of religious revolution. Medieval cities saw the creation of new, more rational and systematic codes of law for their citizens, saw these brought about by and in the interests of a new class, an emergent bourgeoisie. The 'drive for urban autonomy', Bendix observed, created conditions within which that unitary standard of ethics, later observable in Puritan sects, could develop. It is to these fraternal associations of burghers that we should look for the origins of 'a single standard of ethics in all business transactions and the use of community controls to guarantee both personal probity and the reliability of legal procedure'.[9]

The Puritan version of Protestantism stressed the importance of the reputation for trustworthiness even when dealing with non-believers, and encouraged the idea that a man should order *all* his relationships with detachment (including those with his family and neighbourhood) so as not to jeopardize his 'calling'. This emotional detachment helped to reduce the social distance between men, to break down the particularistic ties of kinship and neighbourhood, to make possible the entry of the stranger. The medieval cities of Europe allowed *individual* freedom from feudal obligations, *individual* membership of the citizenry, *individual* participation in a religious association and in doing so became places marked by social heterogeneity, by institutional experiment and by a growing diversity of ideas and beliefs. They provided a context within which a 'rational and inner-worldly ethic' could be developed by those who sought to resolve the specifically political problems of a new status group of merchants and urban *rentiers* struggling to free itself from the traditional secular and religious obligations of feudal society. For Bendix, *The City* provides an historical background for the *Protestant Ethic and Spirit of Capitalism* but, as he acknowledges, the link between the two works was not made explicit by Weber and there are dangers in stressing this particular connection, for

> Like his other studies, Weber's analysis of the city encompasses many different theories, and while I emphasise its relevance for the essays on Protestantism, it is just as legitimate to treat the study as a partial history of Western European democracy.[10]

Indeed it is, and the best treatment of this work is found in the essentially political interpretation offered by Guenther Roth in his introduction to *Economy and Society*,[11] where rather than playing up the ties to *The Protestant Ethic*, he encourages us to look on *The City* as a contribution to Weber's general interest in 'the sociology of domination'.

When Weber spoke of 'domination' (*Herrschaft*) he was at pains to distinguish this from mere power or force (*Macht*). Thus, he wrote:

> In our terminology, domination shall be identical with authoritarian power of command. To be more specific, domination will thus mean the situation in which the manifested will (command) of the ruler or rulers is meant to influence the conduct of one or more others (the ruled) and actually does influence it in such a way that their conduct, to a socially relevant degree, occurs as if the ruled had made the content of the command the maxim of their conduct for its own sake.[12]

which means, as Roth observes, that a system of domination refers to 'a structure of superordination and subordination sustained by a variety of motives and means of enforcement'.[13]

Throughout his academic career, Weber was engaged with two problems. First, the origins and nature of capitalism as they appeared in Antiquity, in the Middle Ages and in modern times; secondly, the structures of domination and social stratification in those ages. *The City* is thus located at the confluence of these two streams of curiosity but it seems to contribute more to the latter than the former, for it documents in great detail the variety of political struggles which took place in the towns and cities of northern and southern Europe from the eleventh to the fifteenth centuries. It depicts the medieval cities as places of revolution, as centres in which legitimate forms of political authority were challenged and overthrown, as places where new classes and strata appeared and contrived first to usurp power and subsequently to establish some legitimation for their own system of rule. These struggles were not mere parochial disputes, because despite considerable differences through time and across societies they represented the piecemeal efforts to transform the economic and political systems that we call feudalism. The efforts of the townsmen to gain autonomy for themselves and their towns, their challenges to the authority of princes, bishops and military rulers were reactions to inconsistencies, complexities and contradictions of feudal society. Where the townsmen succeeded they established a 'state within a state', with their own patrician rulers set up in defiance of traditional rulership, their own oath-bound associations of free men, of 'citizens', whose willingness and ability to fight had brought about the usurpation of power and now defended the new 'non-legitimate' domination. In some places, notably in Italy, these 'revolutions' were followed by others in which the urban patriciate, those noble families whose domination had become well entrenched, were challenged by the growing class of entrepreneurs and craftsmen. A new force, the *'popolo'* appeared and seized control of the towns. In their turn, they too had the problem of consolidating their position, of seeing to it that the dispossessed upper strata did not regain power. Like earlier 'usurpers' they had to construct an administrative apparatus whereby they could secure their positions, gain legitimacy and turn 'power' into effective domination.

Thus, Weber depicts the medieval town as a place of conflict, as an arena in which rival classes and status groups struggled for power, as a place in which the major changes, structural, institutional and ideological, in the wider society produced revolutionary action. It is this sense of the city as a coliseum for political struggle that we most want to take from Weber and apply to our contemporary urban areas.

The city

One of Weber's concerns was to show how the cities of medieval Europe contributed to the uniqueness of the west and he argued that although cities existed and indeed played important roles in the history of other societies, cultures and eras, it was only in Medieval Europe that there emerged what he called 'full urban communities'. To qualify for this description, he claimed the settlement must display a relative predominance of trade-commercial relations, there must be fortifications, a market, some degree of autonomy of law – at least a court of its own. There should be an associational structure *(Verbandscharakter)* and some degree of political autonomy and capacity to establish its own political leaders. And finally, there has to be a system of administration with officers in whose election the burghers participated.[14]

Cities in other civilisations, in India and China for example, had shared many of these characteristics, but always there were ties of caste or clan which prevented the emergence of an estate of economically independent and legally free burghers. The ritual prescriptions of caste, sustaining occupational divisions, a hierarchy of 'purity' and a host of restrictions on social contact in Indian cities, or the overriding loyalty to clan and ancestors perpetuating powerful ties to the countryside in China – these militated against the development of 'full urban communities'. In medieval Europe, Christianity overcame some of the older parochial loyalties, establishing a potential commonality among travellers from diverse parts of the continent and contributing to the increasing freedom from traditional obligations to clan and ritual associations. And the growth of trade from the tenth century on, promoted a great increase in contacts between different regions, cities and individuals. Only in medieval Europe, Weber argues, did there emerge the precise, historical configuration which led to the creation of cities as 'fraternal associations'. Only in Europe did individuals take oaths of loyalty which committed them to defend and promote the interests of their fellow burghers and the institutions of their town. Only in Europe did there appear fraternities of citizens who would repudiate the authority of princes, bishops and nobles and by insidious process or open revolt dismantle the complex structures of feudal power and build their own systems of law, their own fabric of domination.

The expansion of commerce in the medieval period was the great stimulus to the growth of towns. Beginning in the Mediterranean and fueling the development first of the Italian cities, trade grew through the twelfth, thirteenth and fourteenth centuries stretching eastwards to India, south to Africa, west to Spain and north through France, Flanders, Germany and Britain. By the fourteenth century the northern and eastern towns of Germany were booming, as they stimulated and co-ordinated the trade of the North Sea and the Baltic. Goods, mundane and exotic, circulated over a wide area. In a Flanders town in the thirteenth century you might find merchants' inventories recording wine from France, wool from England, grain from Sicily, pepper from Malabar, Indian ginger and Spanish saffron. The medieval period saw the creation of a continental civilisation, a civilisation in which the town was the major agent of change and symbol of development.

The towns of Europe grew up in diverse ways. Some had gathered around a religious house – an abbey or a monastery; others grew up as centres of administration or as garrisons and fortresses. All were markets, but the character of their economic activity could, as Weber showed, vary widely: from the 'consumer' cities where goods were brought in or made to meet the needs of feudal princes and lords, to 'producer' settlements whose economic role was overwhelmingly that of production, of manufacture; or as 'merchant' cities in which profits were made from the purchase, sale and circulation of foreign and domestic commodities. Partly as a result of the complexities of their town's development, the inhabitants were subject not to a unified system of authority, but to a bewildering set of powers:

> Numerous claims to authority stand side by side, overlapping and often conflicting with each other. Episcopal powers of seigneurial and political nature; appropriated vicontiel and other political office powers resting partly on chartered privileges and partly on usurpation; powers of great urban feudatories or freed ministeriales of the king or the bishops *(capitanei);* those of rural or urban subfuedatories *(valvassores)* of the *capitanei,* allodial clan properties of most varied origin; countless owners of castles fortified on their own authority or that of some other power, a privileged estate wielding authority over a broad stratum of clients, either bound or free; occupational unions of the urban economic classes; judicial powers based on manorial law, on feudal law, on territorial law and on ecclesiastic law – all these are found in the same city.[15]

Corresponding to the different social groups there were different systems of law with which they sought to order social relationships and defend their particular interests. Secular and ecclesiastical notables when not residing in the towns still could maintain bondsmen there in order to exploit the possibilities of trade or manufacture. The fact that a prosperous bondsman could be recalled from the town, ordered to boots and saddle service by his lord, if for no other reason than to exort a ransom from him, ensured common interest on the part of many urbanites. They wanted to be free. Free of those overlapping and outmoded 'impositions', free of the irrational systems of establishing truth by ordeal or combat, free from what were increasingly felt to be archaic, anachronistic impositions. The more people travelled, the more foreigners they met in their cities, the more sharply conscious they became of their relative freedom or subjugation. In 1202 the burghers of Tournus petitioned their Burgundian lord to relinquish his control over marriage. The burghers had become sensitive to the jeers of those passing through their town. That the lord still dictated who should marry whom was a source of shame. they resented being laughed at and called serfs.[16]

What was desired by the merchants and the urban nobility was a simplified, unitary code whereby the affairs of men in the city could be ordered. Thus, it was that in the 'true urban communities' those who were committed to rational economic conduct struggled to establish a large measure of autonomy for their towns. They urged the reform of legal institutions and the election or appointment of magistrates and mayors alongside or as replacements for the representatives of traditional feudal superiority. On occasion the struggle for autonomy was won without serious conflict if bishops and princes conceded the claims of the burghers and allowed them to establish separate courts with their own officers, or permitted 'an oath-bound association of citizens' to elect their own leaders who would further the urban interests in trade and commerce. And there were occasions when the feudal superiors could see that it might be in their interests to make such concessions to the townsmen. The princes and nobles might well benefit from the growth of trade and some of their number were, after all, already very much at home in the towns. Especially in the Italian cities there quickly developed an urban nobility and as owners of land and property in the cities, they had a real interest in urban development. In the medieval city, as Mundy and Riesenberg observe: 'Construction was an early source of wealth and many large fortunes were made in it and in real estate.'[17]

But often the concessions were wrung from unwilling superiors who recognized that their authority had already been usurped long before there were any open or public moves for reform, and they acquiesed only because they lacked the force with which to confront an organized and armed citizenry. The townsmen frequently found themselves in open conflict with the church, for while some of the secular lords might have been quick enough to see the material advantages of trade, the ecclesiastical authorities were less enthusiastic about commerce and its common accompaniment, usury. Thus we find townsmen openly revolting against bishops and archbishops: in Milan in 1057, in Worms in 1073 and Cologne in 1288.

Weber argues that the conventional history of these confrontations underplays the genuinely revolutionary character of the bourgeois associations, because all too often the legitimate and peaceful transfer of authority is stressed rather than the acts of usurpation. And that is hardly surprising, for each regime tries to rewrite history in such a way as to establish its legitimacy. These associations of medieval urbanites *were* revolutionary: they seized power and transformed institutions for their own benefit and did so commonly with the use or at least the threat of real violence. Theirs was a non-legitimate domination. It was the domination of a group of propertied burghers over the mass of propertyless artisans and petty traders and casual workers who made up the bulk of the urban population.

Already, from this sketch we can begin to gain some impression of Weber's general analysis. He portrays the development of the urban community as the product of the interests of an emergent burgher class whose unity was forged for and by the battles with their feudal masters. Within the towns, conflicting interests met and the groups representing religious or secular orders each mobilized different resources in their determination to hold or usurp power. Thus, central to the sociological analysis are the *sources* of power. called upon by various groups. There is the property of *rentiers* and that of merchants and traders, there is the military tradition and skills of a knightly class, the technical skills of artisans, the charisma of clergy – all these are sources of power. In England, where the burghers never acquired anything like the autonomy of their counterparts in Germany, it was principally economic power which propertied townsmen were able to exploit in their dealings with the monarch and with parliament. On the continent especially, in less unified kingdoms, the economic base of the burghers was buttressed by real military might. The citizens were armed, and under obligation to police particular quarters of the city, to defend them and sometimes the whole city from attack. And these burgh militias could be mobilized for revolutionary purpose. Indeed, Weber observes, 'All conjurations and city unions of the Occident . . . were coalitions of the armed strata of the cities.'[18]

In the western medieval city, then, the process of 'revolutionary usurpation' met with repeated success. The cities became 'non-feudal islands in a feudal sea', but they were islands with a high degree of connection one to another. Not just the journeyings of the merchants linked them together, but basic economic interdependencies developed, as, for instance, between English towns and those in Flanders, the one supplying and the other finishing English wool. There were connections too between the guilds, with guild organisations formed to tie together members of a given trade in different urban centres. There was even a wholesale 'export' of urban law and related institutions from one town to another. Thus, Weber tells us, 'The burghers of Freiburg received a charter grant of the same law as Cologne. Numerous South German cities were chartered with the law of Freiburg.'[19]

However, while there were factors promoting some kinds of unity among the medieval towns, there were also considerable variations in their development. In the north of Italy, the towns came to dominate the countryside, creating a series of contiguous city states. In Germany and northern Europe, towns attained a high degree of autonomy but they did not rule over extensive territories in the way of their southern counterparts. In France and in England, the monarchy quickly integrated the towns into the developing nation-state.

In Weber's account of medieval cities, we are made sharply aware of the differences between urban centres, especially the diverse ways in which internal political struggles produced different patterns of domination.

The patrician city

Many cities were dominated by an urban nobility or patriciate whose powers, at least initially, rested on landed property and rental income. The noble families had founded many of the urban centres seeing in them prospects of enhancing their wealth through control and encouragement of markets, but though they hoped to prosper from this commerce, their traditional attitude toward the new class of traders whose growth they were sponsoring has been described by

Pirenne:

> the nobility never had anything but disdain for these upstarts come
> from no-one knew where and whose insolent good fortune they
> could not bear. They were infuriated to see them better supplied
> with money than themselves; they were humiliated by being
> obliged to have recourse, in times of trouble to these newly rich.[20]

The noble families had their roots in the country, but over time
some became throughly urbanized, taking up residence in the city,
deriving major slices of their wealth from their urban property and
coming to share with the merchants and entrepreneurs, an interest in
freeing the city from exterior authority. None the less, noble families
remained distinctive. They had landed property, they commanded
military resources, were militarily trained and they maintained a
'knightly' style of life. Weber describes how, in Venice, the noble
families gained control of the city, through their ownership of military
and financial resource. They were the only group able to pay for the
commercial and colonial adventures which led to the eminence of
Venice as a trading city. They closed ranks, ceased to admit outsiders
to their number, demoted the doge and concentrated administration
of the city's affairs in the hands of a few families. They established a
remarkably closed form of patrician domination.

Elsewhere, other noble families were also drawn into the
administration of city life because they too enjoyed the privileges and
liabilities of property ownership and military power. But in most
other Italian cities the noble stratum was not closed, nor was it
internally disciplined in the Venetian fashion. Consequently, several
noble families with their numerous friends, allies and dependent
supporters might confront each other and set up, within the city,
violent and long-lasting feuds. Each 'party' would attempt to
monopolize the administrative offices and sources of wealth and to
transmit these to its descendants, kinsmen and trusted retainers.
Quite often the squabbling factions reduced civic administration to a
shambles and in the thirteenth century there appeared what Weber
calls 'a noble professional officialdom' out of the institution of the
'podestà'. The podestà was elected from among the notables and in
return for a fixed salary he was given the task of establishing effective
administration of the city. He came with his followers and set up a
staff responsible for running the town, guaranteeing its peace and

upholding its law. Thus, there emerged a group of professional administrators, trained in law and using law as an instrument to consolidate and legitimize the rule of patrician families. The most enduring monuments of the podestà were the codified, rational systems of law it propagated.

Martindale suggests that we can see the 'city managers' of more recent times as latter-day versions of the podestà, and it is certainly true that the enthusiasm for 'professionals' being called in to organize municipal affairs has often arisen out of similar suspicions of corruption or complacency among the 'parties' traditionally running a town. The city managers will clean up the corruption, act dispassionately, efficiently, rationally – that at least has been the theory.

Perhaps most important though of all the institutions of these early cities was the 'conjuration' – the oath-bound association of citizens. In the Italian cities the conjuration meant the consolidation of patrician power, furthering their economic ambitions and reinforcing their domination. Within the city the patriciate administered the oath to all those burghers who, through holdings of property, qualified for citizenship. Those who refused to swear the oath were exiled. In this way, the most powerful townsmen were bound together, united in their defiance of outside authority, obliged to defend their city, their livelihood and the new and illegitimate system of law and administration which the patriciate had instituted. The 'conjuration' provided the basis for the greatest degree of city autonomy.

In England the more consolidated power of the monarch and of the nobility ensured that there were no usurpations of this kind. The English cities did not win political independence and juridicial autonomy. Nevertheless, to the monarch, the city was an important source of revenue, and the cities developed an economic rather than political significance. The burghers in English cities were given sole rights to collect taxes, and out of this function they developed in time autonomy of fiscal administration. Private commercial guilds became the guarantors of the city's fiscal obligations, and became the decisive unions in the city, often bestowing citizenship rights. The city as a 'territorial institution' as in Italy never developed in England. It was always bound more tightly to the developing state, its economic significance readily acknowledged and marked by the rights of corporation which were granted. The burghers were granted special privileges within the system of estates, special representation in the 'commons' but they never won more than very limited areas of autonomy for their towns and cities. The representation of specifically urban interests within the national parliament though was important, for it helped promote a measure of integration among the burgher class and this in time would facilitate the growth of a genuinely *national* bourgeoisie.

The plebeian city

The patrician city was one dominated by noble families whose military traditions, life style and sources of economic power set them off from their fellow citizens, the wealthy burghers, who derived their livelihood from trade. The patricians might establish political control of the urban centres with the assistance of the merchants, but the persistence of distinctive material interests and casts of mind sowed the seeds of conflict. The *rentier* nobles often had little respect for the successful burghers. Specifically: 'it was any rational, continuously organised, and in this sense specifically *bourgeois* form of acquisitive operation, any systematic activity, that was looked upon with disdain.'[21] These social, political and economic differences between legally equal citizens resulted in struggles for power *within* the city and the usurpation of patrician domination. The most successful 'revolutions' of this kind occurred in Italy where the rule of noble families was broken by the entrepreneurs and craftsmen – the *'popolo'.* At the beginning of the thirteenth century this 'political sub-community' could be found in Bologna, Siena, Verona, Pavia and other cities. The *popolo* had its origins in a sense of injustice. The noble families were attempting to exclude non-nobles from office or they were denying them legal rights or refusing to pay their debts to the artisans and traders. The *popolo* developed a separate political organisation becoming effectively a state within a state. The entrepreneurs and artisans in their guilds elected a 'captain' of the *popolo*, they provided him with quarters, a staff and a military force. In its fullest form the *popolo* assumed the right to make laws and to press these on the whole urban community. The *podestà* was often forced to come to terms with this parallel administration and, in some instances, to bow to it. It was, says Weber, 'a separate political community within the urban commune with its own officials, its own finances and its own military organisation'.[22]

Weber tells us that where it achieved its greatest power, the *popolo* turned the tables on the nobility, making noble birth the grounds for exclusion from positions of power in the city, restricting their rights under the law and excluding them from office in the guilds. The intellectual support for this new 'revolution' in the cities came typically from the guild-organized 'professionals', like doctors and notaries and pharmacists, and much of the financial support was solicited from the entrepreneurial guilds.

Initially the captain of the *popolo* was elected for a short term, but as with other power holders, some extended their tenure and concentrated more and more authority in their own hands and those of their families. In other cases the *popolo* was supported, encouraged and ultimately manipulated by ambitious noble families. Either way, one development out of the *popolo* was the *'signoria'*, a form of city tyranny. The non-legitimate nature of this domination was plain but the 'tyrants' were able to force the patricians aside, weakening them and extracting concessions and compromises such that relations between noble and commoner were changed for ever. In this way, Weber observed, 'tyranny was frequently the forerunner of democracy'.

Urban autonomy: rise and fall

From Weber's description, then, it is clear that beginning in the eleventh century European cities underwent major political transformations. It is clear too that the changes in the character of the cities, in their political and administrative arrangements, proceeded at different paces and along different pathways in various parts of Europe. However, certain common features can be established.

First, there was the quest for autonomy, most weakly developed in England, substantially developed in Germany but most successfully established in Italy, which transformed urban settlements into free associations of local landlords and property owners. The earliest oath-bound fraternities were small, involving only sections of the community and several conjurations might exist simultaneously within a town, but these soon gave way to city-wide associations which could present concerted opposition to traditional rulers. Their initial objectives might sound modest enough, consisting as they did of the desire to be able to settle disputes amicably within a framework of laws administered by men like themselves, but they were profound in their implications, for they called for nothing less than the sweeping away of old and overlapping feudal jurisdictions and the creation for the city dwellers of a new and more rational system of law. not only that, but they were claiming (though they did not always win) the right to elect magistrates and law officers from their own number and in this way free themselves from judgement and administration by feudal overlords or their personal retainers and agents. The search for reformed and appropriate law even led in some instances to guilds and craft associations creating their own law within the city's revised system.

Alongside this, other ambitions were developed. The burghers sought to monopolize commerce and production, to stimulate and protect trade and ensure that its benefits were not syphoned off by rural landowners. They wanted to raise taxes on their own initiative as well as putting the claims of feudal superiors on a firmer and less arbitrary basis. Tax obligations were to be rationalized, so that they would be more predictable and calculable. And since profit and economic power were derived from city markets, the associations of citizens determined to transfer their administration from the city lord or lords to the new civic authorities or to a licensed 'corporation' of those who dealt in specific goods. Finally, there was the desire to establish an effective militia to defend the town and later, to extend its political and economic influence.

The struggle for autonomy took many forms ranging from agreements with the founders of new towns, which established from the beginning the rights of citizens to their own political and administrative machinery, through piecemeal agreements which wrested these powers from the founders by degrees, to the revolutionary usurpation of authority by an armed and militant conjuration.

The outcomes of these negotiations, surreptitious appropriations or revolts were varied, but in the medieval cities the mayor came to assume the first rank and, unlike magistrates, was always a representative of the citizens. The cities acquired municipal courts and some freedom to enact and administer their own laws. In Italy the cities acquired far more freedom in this respect than their counterparts in northern Europe. Similarly, there were great differences from south to north in the capacities of cities as tax authorities. In England the tax powers of the city were always dependent on and linked to the demands of a monarch for revenue, though considerable powers over specific areas of trade were granted by the king to city corporations. And in the same way we find considerable variation in the military capacity of cities and the extent to which this could be employed autonomously. Only in Italy, most notably in Venice, did there appear city 'states' whose armies and fleets could set out on their own colonial adventures. Elsewhere the military power of the city was used to control its immediate hinterland, to establish urban monopolies and to force the peasants to sell their produce to city markets.

Weber's analysis points to a very special period of urban development in which cities in many parts of Europe enjoyed an extraordinary freedom. For a short while, it seemed that cities really did make men free; the revolutionary movements of citizens brought institutional reform, economic vigour and a ferment of ideas. But it was not to last. Always there was the threat of counter-revolution, the chance that external authority would be reimposed or the possibility that the traditionally privileged groups would find ways of joining the new associations, as some of the nobility did with the guilds, or contrive to subvert the 'revolutions', turning the illegitimately acquired power to their own interests. The 'freedoms' were often fragile. In some cities the guilds turned the burghers' freedom into narrow privilege; in others, elected leaders converted their office into hereditary domination, extending their powers from particular to general and creating a new urban patriciate.

The military strength of the oath-bound associations which had once frightened the lords, secular and ecclesiastical, who could not muster or could not sustain comparable forces, began to decline. The duty to bear arms got in the way of business activity and princes and patricians who could promise to relieve the burghers of these responsibilities by organizing 'plebeian' armies were welcomed. By the sixteenth century, the independent city had everywhere lost ground to more powerful monarchs and princelings and the new authority of the state. Thus, Weber describes a cyclical process for the city: from subordination to feudal or territorial lords, a brief though important autonomy, the decay of that freedom and then the subordination of the city to the patrimonial state. Cities became rich sources of tax revenue for the ambitious monarchs and their courtiers and the control and manipulation of the cities and their corporations was a matter of statecraft. Rorig[23] documents the decline of the old merchant class in German towns, pointing to the way lawyers and others who seemed to have forgotten their burgher origins, joined those nobles supporting the supremacy of princes and the subordination of the towns to the petty states. His analysis highlights the rise of what he calls the 'common bourgeoisie' within these new political formations and underlines the shifting structures of class and status which form an important part of Weber's analysis.

' Ironically, much of the impetus for larger territorial groupings came from the very success of the independent cities with their institutions 'adaptable' to capitalism, for the forms of enterprise they had encouraged outgrew their boundaries:

> The traditional forms of enterprise integrated in the 'city economy' no longer were the ones which could generate the really great profits, and further . . . both the politically oriented and the commercial and industrial capitalist undertakings simply no longer found a useful support in policies of the 'city economy' type . . . Even where these undertakings were formally located in the city, they could no longer be sustained by an entrepreneurdom tied locally to the individual burgher association.[24]

As capitalist activity grew, individual entrepreneurs and their families sought to extend their influences over productive processes, buying and selling over wider and wider areas, co-ordinating supplies from different regions, controlling distribution of the products, developing new markets. In his recent study of Nördlingen, Christopher Friedrichs provides a vivid description of the rise of the Wörner family through precisely these entrepreneurial activities.[25] Step by step the family moved toward overall control of weaving in the town, monopolizing the supply of materials, binding the craftsmen to them through debt and undertaking the marketing of the cloth. The Wörners and their like sought wider and wider territories in which their goods could be sold. They encouraged political and economic unification in much the same way that large corporations very recently have lobbied for bigger marketing areas (like the European Common Market). As the medieval town gave way to the early modern town, so the emerging bourgeoisie threw in their lot with those who sought to undermine the old urban autonomy, who sought to make the towns subordinate elements in new nation-states. Thus, the twin developments, the emergence of the nation-state and that of national capitalism, brought about the decline of the autonomous city. As Weber observed in his *General Economic History:*

> out of the alliance of the state with capital, dictated by necessity, arose the *national* citizen class, the bourgeoisie in the modern sense of the word. Hence, it is the closed national state which afforded capitalism its chance for development.[26]

It was this class which would grow inside the early modern towns and ultimately unchain the extraordinary economic forces that could create the industrial cities and transform the entire world.

Chapter 3

The Emergence of the Modern City

How should we understand the growth of the modern city? Weber's own analysis provides us with several important clues but no sustained exploration of the complex processes whereby those walled settlements with their *'amical leagues'* were transformed into the places we know today. It is the purpose of this chapter to provide a sketch, and in so brief a space it will necessarily be a very rough sketch, of the two processes of world-historical significance which guided the transition from the independent urban centres of the medieval period to the so-called 'corporate' cities of the west in the late twentieth century. In doing so we shall need to look at the emergence of the *modern state* and the concurrent *development of capitalism*. As we do this, we can see why it is important to locate the cities within the wider struggles for rulership and also to explore the ways in which changing social structures in the cities have led to sequential shifts in the bases of social action and social conflict.

Cities and the growth of the modern state

In the previous chapter we used Weber's arguments to show that medieval towns were associated with and partially responsible for the switch from 'feudalism' to a new form of political arrangement, a form best described as the *Standestaat* or 'the polity of the Estates'. This system of rule was based upon the dual authority of the territorial rulers and those corporate groups of feudal nobles, clergy and townsmen who came together in parliaments and various assemblies of estates.[1] The territorial ruler and these representative groupings met to exercise power over the great mass of the population and in their deliberations, the townsmen most often sided with the territorial ruler for increasingly it was his authority which upheld the peace and established a framework of law which furthered the development of their interests. As central authority expanded, with smaller territories being absorbed into larger ones, so the ruler's administrative apparatus grew larger and more sophisticated and his capacity to exploit differences within and between the estates enabled him, step by step, to assert his supremacy within this polity. Gradually the powers of the estates waned, the townsmen's along with those of feudal lords and clergy, and monarchs came to exert more and more influence over those who had once claimed to share rulership with them.

In the early modern period of the sixteenth and seventeenth centuries in England we can see some evidence of this. The nature of urban politics in the early modern towns was largely determined by the royal charters which defined the specific areas of civic autonomy and the rights and duties of privileged elites. Charters gave the cities their own courts, their own justices of the peace and rights to control much of their commercial, industrial and financial life. The 160 charters granted to English towns between 1500 and 1700 provided the legal and fiscal frameworks whereby local elites could maintain public order in the interests of wealthy minorities.

But the charters also served to specify the relationship between the city and the wider polity and throughout this period, we can see how the monarchy exploited urban dissension, granting, withholding and modifying charters in ways which suited the central authority. Charters of incorporation were powerful instruments for the extension of monarchical power. As Clark and Slack describe them, charters were

> Treaties of alliance between a crown which wished to see power in the hands of a group small and rich enough to be answerable to it and urban elites determined to perpetuate their local status.[2]

Power in the cities was becoming increasingly concentrated. In the sixteenth century, many cities experienced decline of traditional industries, high inflation and consequent indebtedness. Those very wealthy families and individuals prepared to loan the city money and to accept civic office could secure for themselves, their kin and their friends a large measure of control over urban affairs. Small groups of the richest citizens circulated the civic offices amongst themselves and contrived the exclusion of those they deemed unfit to rule. The guilds having been weakened by the growing diversity of their members' economic activities, by the breakdown of the traditional specificity of trade or craft, found their highest offices 'usurped' by the wealthy oligarchy that already occupied the positions of civic authority. Even members of the gentry might find it expedient to use the guild structure as an avenue of access to urban power.

There was nothing new in the intermeshing of civic and guild offices. In Coventry, for instance, in the early sixteenth century, we are told that: 'Some years after being sheriff, a man became master of the Corpus Christi Guild; then, after a short gap, mayor; and finally, master of the Trinity Guild.'[3] What was new was that the guild structures gradually served less as means of protecting the interests of a broad group of craftsmen, or as vehicles for the expression of religious and communal solidarity and more as buttresses of oligarchic power.

The tendencies to exclusivity in urban politics provoked periodic unrest among the citizenry and among some of those in the ranks of the unfree, and concessions were made in the form of expanded councils or second chambers of the urban legislatures, but mostly these were cosmetic treatments, the real decisions still being made by an 'inner circle' of the urban elites. The simmering discontents became resources for the monarchy, providing excuses for intervention in civic affairs, revisions of charters and a general extension of crown influence. The aldermanic cliques needed the support of the central authority and its agents; the monarchy and the local gentry who served as its 'field officers' wanted to be able to affect what went on in the towns. Towns, after all, were dangerous places, nurturing ideas of dissent and sedition.

By the end of the seventeenth century the subordination of the towns within a wider, more centralized polity was unequivocal, but the form of central control in England, the supremacy of Parliament following the rejection of the Stuart claims to absolutism, was unusual. Elsewhere, kings ruled from the growing and glittering courts (as in France) or through an elaborate bureaucratic apparatus (as in eighteenth-century Prussia).[4] In all cases, though, it was clear that the old authority of the estates, including the towns, was now eclipsed. Absolutism or other forms of central rule had supplanted the *Standestaat* and the towns were absorbed into a much wider and more potent complex of domination.

But the unification of territories and the growth of monarchical power did more than simply reduce the towns' autonomy or their rights to share in the exercise of power. The growth of central authority gave impetus to the development of great capitals, cities housing the royal household and court and all the principal institutions of law, justice and administration. Cities like Paris and London reflected this and in England (much more so than in France) the political and economic integration of the country fostered the growth of regional centres. In the early modern period the provincial capitals, though they certainly experienced the ravages of disease and fire and the fluctuations of trade, though they undoubtedly lost a good deal of their individuality, none the less grew in influence. Cities like York, Exeter, Bristol, Newcastle and Norwich benefited from their positions as centres of that long-distance trade, encouraged by the mercantilist policies of the monarchs. Especially in the latter years of the seventeenth century, the merchant adventurers and other traders extended their economic influence in the Baltic, in southern Europe and across the Atlantic. Culturally too, the regional centres grew in stature, their grammar schools and petty schools, their cathedrals and minsters and churches symbolizing their importance as the centres of knowledge – secular and sacred, established and dissenting.

Meanwhile, many ancient county and market towns in England had undergone serious decline, but this was in some measure offset by the emergence of new towns. Some like Manchester and Birmingham grew as industrial centres, others like Portsmouth and Chatham were dockyard towns whose prosperity rested on military needs and colonial adventures, and a third set, the spa towns like Tunbridge and Bath and Epsom, provided diversion for those with wealth and leisure.[5]

The seventeenth and eighteenth centuries in Europe saw the rise of powerful states whose rulers were eager to expand their territories and their wealth. In order to swell the coffers of the central power, they sought to extend their empires and through colonial trading and the taxation of their citizens, to add to the glamour and the glory of their courts. In their quests for wealth, they stimulated mercantile activity, doing so in a fashion which ensured a large measure of central control over patterns of commerce, over systems of production, even over wages. But the economic expansion brought with it changes in the mode of production and it stimulated the growth of a sizeable and increasingly diversified bourgeoisie, some sections of which came to experience the 'protective' devices of mercantile capitalism as serious limitations on their own economic activity. By the end of the eighteenth century, there were strong pressures for new political arrangements, arrangements which would enable the *industrial* bourgeoisie to pursue their distinctive economic interests and to shape the apparatus of the state to their own ends.

The impetus for reform (or indeed for revolution) came from a bourgeoisie that had emerged as a *class*, a collectivity linked not by a sharply differentiated and legally confirmed style of life but simply by a common market position. Two particular sections of this class did most to formulate criticism of the old regimes. First and most obviously, the *industrial* bourgeoisie who found much to object to in the established patterns of patronage and privilege and second, those engaged in intellectual literary and artistic pursuits who, through their societies and meeting places, their pamphlets and journals, came to constitute a series of questioning publics which dared to scrutinize and criticize their rulers. Poggi suggests that there emerged a vision of a new constitutional design of the state in which a 'reasoning public' would steer and control its affairs:

> The public realm – once constituted as an elected assembly placed at the very centre of the state – would serve that constituency and activate the state on its behalf by framing as general and abstract laws the prevalent orientations of opinion on given issues as reflected in the formation of majorities and minorities among the elected representatives.[6]

Among those 'prevalent orientations of opinion', of course, were the economic, political, and moral predelictions of the rising bourgeois class.

In the process of creating the 'new' state , those instruments of government by which urban life was directed had also to be reformed, made compatible with the new means of governance that were emerging at the centre. Thus, the reform of the municipal corporations and the establishment of new structures of rule in place of the frequently ramshackle assemblages of ancient manorial and parochial devices served to redefine the place of the towns in the new constitutional state that emerged in Britain in the nineteenth century. The new city governments facilitated much more detailed and direct control of city life by Westminster and Whitehall. As we shall see, the *appearance* of local autonomy was retained and the ideal of 'city patriotism' remained a powerful motif and rallying cry, but in reality, as the state pressed for uniform standards of sanitation and measures of public health and later, as it accepted a measure of public responsibility for housing and welfare, so it accumulated more precise and powerful instruments of central rule. In recent years – during the Heath government and again under Thatcher – the capacity of the state to coerce local authorities to follow the economic and other policies of the central government has been amply demonstrated.

Hopefully, we have said enough to make it plain that in order to understand the development of the cities in the west, it is necessary to see how they fared under at least three distinctive patterns of rule: under the *Standestaat,* under absolutism (or Parliament and Monarch in Britain) and latterly, under the constitutional state.[7]

From burgher to bourgeois: the rise of a capitalist class

We can turn now to the second broad process that moulded the cities, their populations, institutions and spatial structures: to the development of capitalism. Perhaps the simplest way to discuss this protracted and enormously complex process is to focus on the ways in which the 'estate' of burghers in the medieval cities, was transformed into a national, indeed, latterly, an international *class* we call the bourgeoisie.

As we have seen, inside the early modern towns of Europe, social, economic and political relationships were changing. The old solidarity of the citizens or burghers, that propertied and privileged stratum of merchants and artisans, was disintegrating. There had always been considerable differences of wealth within this group but there was a fundamental factor uniting them – their economic independence. The merchants and property holders and wealthy artisans were men of substance with the capacity to produce or trade on their own account, and the legal and political institutions of the cities and the guilds had long functioned to protect them. Throughout the sixteenth and seventeenth centuries, though, this solidarity began to break down as economic and social differentiation of the burghers developed.

The process has been splendidly documented for a German town by Friedrichs[8] who sets out to show how the craftsmen of Nördlingen lost their economic independence and came to constitute, along with the shopkeepers, petty traders and minor officials, a distinct petite bourgeoisie. At the centre of the analysis is the increasing dependence of the artisans and craftsmen on the capitalist merchants. The device which robbed the artisans of their independence was the 'Verlag' or putting-out system found in the textile and in other trades. Gradually, a small number of merchants established control over the supply of raw materials and over the distribution and sale of finished products and they did this by promoting the permanent indebtedness of the craftsmen. There was nothing unusual in artisans borrowing money or materials from a merchant, but mostly this was a short-run affair and so long as the craft guild was strong, the relationship between the producer and the lender-cum-organiser of trade was carefully regulated. However, as the guilds were weakened and as the power of wealthy merchants grew, so it became possible to exploit the debt relationship and for merchants to bind craftsmen to them and to extend their control over markets and resources. Craftsmen could complain of being 'enslaved'. Periods of rapid economic growth with accompanying expansion of credit followed by sharp contractions in demand provided ideal circumstances in which capitalist entrepreneurs could bring about this subjugation of previously independent citizens.

The effect, Friedrichs argues, was not the 'proletarianisation' of the artisans but the formulation of an increasingly distinctive stratum. As they were excluded from positions of economic and political influence, as their prospects of social mobility shrank, so the artisans aligned themselves with the growing number of shopkeepers, petty traders and office holders. They sought to restrict entry to their trades from the ranks of the poor, and tried, by various exclusionary devices, to establish their status superiority *vis-à-vis* the urban proletariat. Thus, by the beginning of the eighteenth century, it was possible to see the replacement of a burgher status group by a differentiated bourgeois class consisting of a relatively well-defined petite-bourgeoisie dominated by and dependent upon a group of capitalist entrepreneurs who held the capital necessary to set or sustain productive activities in progress.

But this kind of social change within cities was very far from uniform. The speed of change and the precise constellation of occupations, strata and classes that emerged varied enormously depending on the patterns of internal and international trade, the state of the rural economy and the nature of the political order – both national and international. In England the late medieval and early

modern period was generally a difficult one for the towns and cities.
There are numerous accounts of public buildings lying unused and
falling into decay, of houses unoccupied, of wealthy families and
individuals refusing civic office and taking themselves off to the
countryside, and always accounts of poverty. In the 1520s the
unemployed and underemployed might account for almost half the
population of a town like Coventry and many of those who were in
jobs lived close to destitution. At the other end of the spectrum there
were those, like the frequently cited Spring family of Lavenham,
Suffolk, who owned 37 per cent of the taxable wealth of the town in
1524. In all the urban centres, there appeared to be very high
concentrations of wealth and even in the later, more prosperous years,
the problems of providing relief for the numerous poor remained
formidable.

However, throughout the period, the social composition of the
towns altered. The urban centres themselves became more
specialized in their economic functions (those that failed to do so
experienced serious decline) and if they lost some of their industrial
capacities to the rural areas they expanded quite noticeably the array
of services they offered. Shopkeeping became a more common
occupation as dealers established relatively permanent sites instead
of trading in the traditional markets. Lawyers, doctors and
apothecaries became more numerous and there were teachers for the
newly founded schools. And increasingly, the gentry came to town.
They came for their clothes and supplies of fashionable items, they
came to avail themselves of professional services, they came for
recreation and enjoyment – and some of them came to stay. They
brought with them both capital and a life style. Their capital served to
stimulate the growth of the service occupations and invigorate the
market for urban land and housing: their life style provided a cultural
template for the professional groups.

Within the towns, there emerged powerful oligarchies of merchants
and aristocrats, men whose interest lay less in the administration and
defence of their particular towns than in the exploitation of trading
opportunities over wider and wider territories. They were bound
together not by oaths of loyalty to the city, they acknowledged no
responsibility to bear arms to defend the place, they were linked
primarily by their common class position as the holders of capital, the
mobilisers of raw material and free labour. In order to expand their
profits, they were anxious to extend the boundaries of foreign trade

and in this they had the backing of ambitious monarchs for whom such trade provided the basis of state power.[9] As this mercantile bourgeoisie developed within the towns of sixteenth-, seventeenth– and eighteenth-century Britain, their activities, in business, leisure and domestic life, gave rise to a host of new services and a great expansion of 'supportive', 'supplementary' occupations. The social structures of the towns were becoming markedly more differentiated.

A network of cities whose dominant groups were committed to long-distance trade helped sustain England as the premier mercantilist power of the late seventeenth and eighteenth centuries.[10] Towns like Bristol, Liverpool and Glasgow became the nodes of a world-wide commerce. Their populations swelled, their wealth increased as a consequence and they began to establish their domination over large regions surrounding them. Thus, Glasgow grew from relative insignificance to a major British city on the basis of its trade connections with the Americas, mainly in tobacco and cotton. As one historian has observed:

> The expansion of transatlantic commerce was crucial to the emergence of the West-central region to a dominating position in the Scottish economy . . . and raised Glasgow from the status of a provincial centre to that of a great international port with developed links through the nexus of European and Atlantic trade.[11]

And these changing economic patterns had social and cultural consequences. Inside these towns, a more finely graduated occupational structure together with the establishment of schools and colleges meant that there were more opportunities for social mobility. The social system appeared rather more 'open'. In the case of Glasgow, for instance, it has been argued that its growth as a great trading centre owed much to such a relatively 'open' structure and to 'a tradition of thorough mercantile education for the aspiring trader'.[12]

The major British cities, then, in the seventeenth and eighteenth centuries were above all places of trade, not of manufacture. Their merchant adventurers combined their wealth to sponsor voyages of exploration and colonisation; they and their representatives travelled far and wide establishing a network of social relationships the length and breadth of Britain, reaching out through its colonies to remote parts of the globe. The merchants sought suppliers of raw materials, dealers to set up outlets for their exotic imports or for finished goods and yet others to supply additional capital. Their webs of social and economic relations grew until they enmeshed even the smallest communities in England, Wales and Scotland. Gone were those rather parochial 'burghers'; they had been replaced by a national bourgeoisie.

The growth of these mercantile centres and their expanding bourgeois elements were important aspects of the economic impact of cities on their hinterlands, their appetite for agricultural products, for manufactured goods, for money, for labour, laid the foundations of a nation-wide, integrated economy.

London, as the city which for centuries had been by far the largest settlement and now stood as the heart of an empire, exerted the most profound influence on the economic and cultural life of the society. Its huge population required vast quantities of food which had to be drawn from an increasingly wider area. Thus, improvements in transportation were called for as too were increases in agricultural productivity. Such a large and growing market encouraged specialisation, not just in the growing of crops and raising of animals, but also in all the tasks associated with their processing, distribution and sale. Similarly, all these thousands of households in the capital needed fuel and again it can be argued there were improvements in transportation and in the technology of mining which flowed from this.

By 1700 London's population was 575,000 making it the largest city in Europe. In the next hundred years, it continued to grow rapidly: 675,000 by 1750, 900,000 by the start of the nineteenth century. In a celebrated article, Wrigley[13] has tried to trace the demographic, cultural, but above all, the *economic* impact of this metropolitan development. One way of thinking about London's influence, he suggests, is simply to estimate the population required (given seventeenth- and eighteenth-century death rates) to sustain the kind of numerical growth the capital enjoyed in these years. London absorbed 'the natural increase of a population of some two-and-a-half millions'. It swallowed up the natural increase of the Home Counties and the Midlands, half the population of England. Of course, in practice, people come to London, not just from those two areas, but from all over the country and from the continent too, and because many migrants subsequently left the capital to go to new districts or return to their home towns and villages, it is reasonable to assume, as Wrigley does, that London's cultural influence must have been very widely spread, that it must have acted as a 'solvent' to traditional attitudes and mores in all corners of the land. It is an important point. It hints at the development of a specifically cultural unification of the society which accompanied political centralisation and economic integration.

As the population of London grew, access to that market became a matter of increasing concern to provincial manufacturers and merchants and their enthusiasm for new roads and canals was an indication of this. By the end of the eighteenth century, there was developed an infrastructure which not only allowed much freer movement of commodities but also made possible the mobility and integration of a bourgeois class. By the beginning of the nineteenth century there had been created a *national* market for goods and services and a numerous *national* bourgeois class. All the trading and dealing laid the foundations of a good many fortunes and it was these accumulations of capital, generated out of mercantile capitalism and supplemented by the wealth of traditional landowners, that were mobilized in the next transformation of society: in the process we like to call the Industrial Revolution.

The triumph of the industrial bourgeoisie

Industrialisation in Britain was accompanied by a massive redistribution of the population. Urban centres grew, especially during the second and third decades of the nineteenth century, at unprecedented rates:

> In 1750, there had been only two cities in Britain with more than 50,000 inhabitants – London and Edinburgh; in 1801 there were already eight; in 1851, twenty-nine including nine over 100,000. By this time more Britons lived in the town than in the country, and almost one-third of Britons lived in cities over 50,000 inhabitants.[14]

Thus Hobsbawm sums up the breakneck urbanisation in which towns like Leeds, Manchester, Birmingham, Liverpool, Glasgow and many others experienced such influxes of population that there was no chance that the burgeoning population could be decently housed or supplied with other basic amenities. The problems of disease, squalor and overcrowding in the industrial slums of Britain have been well documented[15] but behind the physical inadequacies lay the basic fact that the towns lacked the institutional development necessary to govern their inhabitants and order their environments. Some, like Manchester and Birmingham, were not even incorporated towns at the time of the Municipal Corporation Act of 1835. Thus, despite their population size (in 1831 Manchester had 227,808, Birmingham 146,986) they were still operating with governmental machinery which was an antiquated assembly of manorial and parochial institutions, which were dominated, here as elsewhere, by a mixture of landed gentry and wealthy, propertied members of the urban elite. Others, like Leeds, were incorporated but still were ruled by conservative oligarchies of merchants and gentry.

It was these burgeoning industrial centres, having outstripped their machinery of government, which became the prime battlefields on which the landed gentry and established urban elites sought to drive off the challenge from a growing bourgeoisie linked more or less directly with the development of an industrial economy. The struggle for power, and ultimately domination, took many forms but we can think first about the tussles for control over existing political institutions. In nineteenth-century cities, especially prior to 1835, struggles to exercise influence over local expenditure and administration were carried on in the various parochial bodies, the most important of which, because it had tax powers, was the Vestry. The first thirty years or so of the nineteenth century saw the vestries becoming increasingly politicized 'by men whose political ambitions were frustrated elsewhere'.[16] It is important to recognize that there were several points of access to local political systems and that the new men of business, large and small, tried sometimes alone, but often with the help of skilled workers and artisans, to capture vestries and churchwardenships and thereby some control over finance, nominations for administrative and some judicial offices and administration of the Poor Law. Fraser paints a vivid picture of the noisy, rumbustious public meetings in the vestries, their 'beer garden atmosphere', where many who did not meet the property qualifications none the less attended and influenced appointments and policies. Vestries became, in many cases, the prime source of opposition to the oligarchies which ran the industrial towns.

The major struggles were fought out at a national level over the issues of Parliamentary Reform, and at the local level over the matters of Municipal Reform and Incorporation. Many of the wool merchants, textile producers or metal magnates who threw their energies into the Parliamentary Reform movement hoped, indeed, with some reason, expected, that the government plans for Municipal Reform in 1835 would not only give the new bourgeoisie access to local politics but at the same time would equip those large towns which still lacked any charter, with coherent systems of government. They were disappointed. After the Parliamentary Session of 1837, Birmingham and Manchester were still unincorporated. The confrontation between old and new orders was sharpened.

To the rising bourgeoisie the old system of local rule, and indeed, the wider structures of domination, were illegitimate since they restricted power over the most important institutions to a handful of families who made up the mercantile elite or allowed landed gentry to continue in the enjoyment of what, in essence, were residues of feudal power. The new men sought to reform parochial institutions and the structure of local government so as to include those like themselves: men of some substance, men with property, (albeit modest) men who had enjoyed some measure of material success in the world. When some of them found themselves still excluded from political participation even after the Municipal Reform Act, their sense of indignation was well expressed by Cobden:

> The battle of our day is still against the aristocracy . . . The lords of Clumber, Belvoir and Woburn, although they can no longer storm your town, and ransack your stores and shops, at the head of their mailed vassals, are as effectively plundering your manufacturers and their artisans; for, by the aid of their parchment votes and tenants-at-will serfs, they are still enabled to levy their infamous bread tax upon your industry . . . imitate your forefathers by union and cooperation; amalgamate all ranks in your town, by securing to all classes a share in its government and protection; give unity force and efficiency to the intelligent and wealthy community of Manchester, and qualify it by your organisation as it already is entitled by numbers to be the leader in the battle against monopoly and privilege. In a word, INCORPORATE YOUR BOROUGH.[17]

The issue of Incorporation was a potent one in mobilizing townspeople against the existing urban elites for its appeal could reach right down to the working class. Anti-gentry feeling especially was easily stirred among the liberal working men. Thus, the aspiring bourgeoisie could seek allies among sections of the working class and incorporate them, ideologically, in their confrontation with the older order. By 1839 the clamour of the middle class in the industrial cities of Birmingham and Manchester was heeded, charters were granted and the domination, that is to say the *legitimate* exercise of power by the new bourgeois elements was under way.

It is important to keep in mind that the struggles for control of the towns and the reform of their instruments of government were part and parcel of a wider contest. Cities were substantial concentrations of economic power, 'centres of investment matrices',[18] sites of capital accumulation and provided seats from which influence might be exercised over a wider area, but conflicts here were also reflections of conflicts being played out on a national stage, conflicts which had many facets or dimensions. For instance, in the late eighteenth and early nineteenth century, the rejection of the traditional privilege and patronage of the landed interests and the mercantile oligarchies found expression in religion as well as politics. Indeed, it was often difficult to disentangle religious and political conflicts for, in the case of the towns particularly, we find that both kinds are expressed in terms of struggles over the same institutions. As part of their rejection of the 'old order' there were many who foresook the Established Church, the Church of Scotland, as well as the Church of England, and joined or established a 'dissenting' congregation. Religious 'deviance' was one very important voice for reform. Methodists, Congregationalists, Quakers and Scottish 'Free' Churches drew support principally from those who were in some way connected with the 'new' world of industry and commerce – which meant artisans and miners and quarrymen as well as the entrepreneurs, the bourgeois elements making their livings from industrial production. Time and again we discover in the historical studies that major economic alignments in the towns, as well as political alignments, ran parallel to these religious divisions. In Bristol, for example, quite late in the century, we read of conflict between two economic 'blocs' in the city: the old Society of Merchant Venturers which was largely Anglican and Tory confronting the 'new men' involved in the Bristol Chamber of Commerce or the Free Port Association who were mostly non-conformists.[19] Or better still, we find in Gilbert's study, *Religion and Society in Industrial England,* a specific reference to the fact that those seeking control of one of the traditional institutions of government, the Vestry, might do so in the first instance as an expression of religious dissent but soon translate their religious interest into an overtly political one:

> The Church–Chapel rivalry from the 1830s onwards was in fact part of a broad current of social change. The men who took over Vestry meetings in the late 1830s were the same people who gained access to municipal office as a result of the Municipal Corporations Act of 1835; and in many places the old municipal oligarchies consciously used their power to levy church rates as a weapon against the 'usurpers' of power in their municipalities.[20]

Throughout the nineteenth century, religious divisions continued to play an important part in urban life. The 'Church and King' mobs which had attacked Dissenters in the eighteenth century disappeared but there were periodic outbursts of civil disobedience with Dissenters jailed for refusing to pay church rates in 1859–60, there was much vigorous pressure-group politicking over the provisions of the Education Bills of 1870 and 1902, and over Temperance. Though the government of cities became progressively detached from those parochial, church-based institutions that had for so long provided mechanisms of rule, none the less, churches and chapels remained for a long while 'political bases' from which religious groups organized their campaigns for influence and for power in the municipality. After the migrations from Ireland, the Catholic church had this function in some places and in a town like Belfast, the sectarian battles that accompanied elections in the 1830s provided awful evidence of the salience of religious identification.[21]

Religion then played an important part in the conflicts that occurred in nineteenth-century cities, serving, in some ways, to underpin the discontents of these bourgeois groups at the time excluded from political power and providing a mechanism for linking their ambitions and hopes to those of a good many artisans and some among the industrial proletariat. Flowing, as they did, *across* class lines, the currents of religious dissent gave a broad base to the 'new' bourgeois elements in their quest for power. And once established, the dominance of the industrial bourgeoisie could be sustained, at least in part, by religious ideas that enjoined thrift, hard work and self-help and conceded legitimacy to the new political arrangements at the level of state or municipality and those 'fit and proper persons' who claimed the right to rule.

After 1835, the influence of the new bourgeois elements could be seen in the composition of many councils, though in some places, Leeds, for instance, the differences between the old and the new regimes were not immediately apparent if one simply looked at occupational status. The old Corporation, Hennock tells us, was made up of 'leading merchants and professional men with an admixture of outstanding manufacturers'[22] and the new Corporation looked remarkably similar, 'as if the opposing team had gone in to play'.[23] But beneath the occupational similarities there were real differences. The Reform Party was made up of men who were dissenters both in religion and in politics and the leaders had acquired their wealth only recently. None of the old, established merchant families were in their ranks.

Gaining access to local political office had a real significance. It was a means of registering and enhancing the social prominence of those who already enjoyed a measure of economic success (it involved, as Garrard has shown,[24] a good deal of personal expense) and thus was a game played principally by those who were content to be where they were, who had in their own estimation 'arrived'. Those who held office had opportunities to influence the physical growth of the town in ways which might guarantee the exclusivity of some of the wealthier or more desirable districts and the sharply differentiated social areas of Victorian districts bear witness to the hierarchic sensibilities of the nineteenth-century city fathers.[25] Being elected to the council gave power over local taxation and the distribution of public funds, whether for relief of the poor or the maintenance of roads or the construction or purchase of water and gas supplies. It afforded, in short, a measure of control over the local economy, a rich source of contacts and particularly for builders and developers, the possibility of contracts from fellow councillors or from the municipality itself.[26]

By the middle of the last century, the new bourgeois elements had achieved their positions of dominance and the municipalities as well as the state were recast in ways which would ensure that their interests, cultural, social and economic were supreme.

Bourgeois domination and legitimacy

The struggle for domination involves not simply the quest for political

or economic power, but the cultural and social subordination of a
population, and in the industrial towns of Victorian Britain there is
ample evidence of the ways in which specifically bourgeois
domination was accomplished. We see it in the physical structure of
the towns where the cultural impact of industrialism stamped itself on
the streets and houses. As Raymond Williams says:

> These were cities built as places of work; physically in their
> domination of mills and engines, with smoke blackening the
> buildings and effluents blackening the rivers; socially in their
> organisation of homes – 'housing' – around the places of work, so
> that the dominant relation was always there.[27]

The 'culture of the factory' was most marked in one-industry towns
like some of the Lancashire textile centres where deference and
quiescence were contrived through the manufacturers' dominance of
all the principal institutions of the town and their successful
dissemination of ideas and practices supportive of their operations.[28]
In such places, working-class rituals of loyalty and community were
appropriated by party politics, and working-class Toryism with its
celebration of Empire, Nation, Monarchy and Town was often the
dominant political ideology.

Victorian cities were places not of 'freedom' but of 'control', places
in which a growing industrial proletariat had to be subjected to a
rigorous discipline[29] exercised through diverse institutions.
Educational establishments served as a means of regulating and
shaping those who might otherwise pose some threat to the new order.
Industrial schools were set up to engineer the moral improvement
and conformity of dangerous elements in the working class and their
purpose and achievements were sometimes revealed in the ingenuous
accounts of contemporary writers:

> Look round and notice how clean and neat they are. Their hands
> and faces have been well washed, and their hair carefully combed
> and dressed. Their general deportment is at once natural and
> modest; so much do they seem improved, that one is disposed to ask
> if they are indeed the debris of human society – the outcasts that
> haunted the streets extorting charity, imposing on the credulity of
> the benevolent – from a state of hopeless wretchedness and utter
> degradation they have been rendered blooming and obedient.

They now take delight in serving and assisting each other, and the hardest work in the house is the most sought after.[30]

The churches too played their part. In Scottish cities the most stern, most Calvinistic gospel was often espoused by the new industrial and commercial elites who pressed for an austere orderliness in their cities, for the removal of 'nuisances': 'low theatres, sabbath drinking shops, brothels and such attractions'.[31] Prominent Scottish churchmen opposed the New Poor Law in part because it seemed to them to weaken the strict moral control of the Kirk over the poor and workless and for long after that reform the ideas of devout Presbyterian members of the middle class enjoined the exercise of 'relief' in ways which would encourage the habits of work, sobriety and thrift. Poor relief and the regimes of the workhouses were used to 'discipline' the proletarians.

In the industrial cities where the hegemony of a single manufacturer or even a small group of bourgeois families was impossible, the identification of the working class with the ideals of the dominant class was sought in 'triumphalist' politics and the cultivation of civic pride:

> the special significance of civic ritual seems to have lain in [the] notion of a corporate town identity. The fostering of the idea of identified interests was apparent in the ceremonial openings of the great Northern town halls, such as the Rochdale opening in 1867, and the no less splendid Manchester occasion in 1877.[32]

'Town patriotism' was an ideology which sought to incorporate the workers in a complex of values and interests which obscured their subjugation and encouraged their support for the grandiose schemes of the manufacturers and professionals who ran their towns. Cities like Bradford or Leeds symbolized the progress, power and pride of their ruling groups in the construction of elaborate and expensive public buildings. As Briggs observes:

> The Town Hall was to be visible proof that 'in the ardour of mercantile pursuits the inhabitants of Leeds have not omitted to cultivate the perception of the beautiful and a taste for fine arts'. It was to serve as a 'lasting monument of their public spirit and generous pride in the possession of their municipal privileges'.[33]

In the mid-Victorian period, we find that large-business proprietors appear as the most numerous or most influential group among the councillors. Their legitimacy rested firmly on their financial expertise, on their proven ability to 'run a business'. If the chief task of the city fathers was the husbanding of corporate property, then those with experience of owning and managing capitalist enterprises might appear pre-eminently qualified to run the urban centres. Towns, it was argued, were best run by those who had the qualifications for civic office, which is to say those who were 'respectable', who were 'men of substance' and who were 'intelligent'. But wealth and self-assurance often encouraged such men to commit the municipal treasuries to massive expenditures. Their schemes of urban 'improvement' led in many places to financial crises which stimulated opposition. Meeting the costs of the magnificent town halls or the provision of better lighting or roads meant only one thing –higher rates. In Hennock's phrase[34] the local authorities became 'engines of direct taxation' and when the tax burdens escalated there was protest from the smaller property owners who made up the bulk of tax-payers. There emerged a pattern of confrontation between 'expenders' and 'economists' (observable in a good many towns by the latter part of the century) in which the larger bourgeois elements found themselves challenged by the local petite bourgeoisie. Having ousted the old urban oligarchies in the early years of the nineteenth century, the substantial manufacturers and their allies now found that from time to time they were opposed – and indeed defeated – by combinations of bourgeois elements in which the small-business proprietors were numerous and influential.

The interest in 'economy' was not confined to one class or stratum, nor to one party. There were always some large-property owners alongside the small traders and workshop owners but the quest for 'economy' did frequently have the effect of mobilizing and politicizing the lower middle class, the 'shopocracy' who often argued that the big bourgeoisie were 'hardly the proper guardians of the interest of the small tradesmen, heavily rated for their shops, whose savings were often invested in a house or two'.[35] They began to challenge the legitimacy of the larger-business proprietors as the 'natural' leaders in the local polity.

The importance of the petit-bourgeois struggles for local political power varied considerably from one town to another and they were not neatly confined to one period of the nineteenth century. They can only be properly understood in the context of the specific histories of individual cities. However, at the risk of some over simplification, we can say that in the last quarter of the nineteenth century and the early years of this century, local politics in many British cities bore the imprint of petit-bourgeois interests and three commonly occurring legitimatory motifs: 'economy', 'localism' and 'non-partisanship'.

The concern with 'economy' and particularly for parsimony in local government were themes continually emphasized by small-business owners and lower-class ratepayers in the nineteenth century, and were readily intelligible in terms of the material circumstances of their lives. Sudden sizeable increases in rates posed then, as now (just think of all the ratepayers' protests in recent years), real threats to the livelihoods of many who ran 'marginal' businesses and strained the family budget of many a white-collar worker who had bought himself a flat or house. Though they may have identified in many ways with the larger entrepreneurs, the small-business owners could never completely escape some awareness of their dependency upon the bigger enterprises and that could be considerably sharpened if the major business owners on the council embarked on ambitious and expensive schemes of civic improvement. Thus, the petit-bourgeois elements often constituted important elements within the Economy Parties or sent some of their number to the town halls as 'ratepayer' councillors delegated to put a brake on the schemes of the expenders.

'Localism', the insistence that municipal affairs be run by local people with local knowledge, was long established and was appealed to by both radicals and Conservatives among the small-business stratum. There were several justifications for this view. It could be argued that keeping the control of municipal affairs in the hands of locals made for efficiency, minimized extravagance and ensured that those who paid the piper also called the tune. We find both ideas in the Report of the Royal Sanitary Commission in 1871:

> The principle of local self government has been generally recognised as of the essence of our national vigour. Local administration under central superintendence, is the distinguishing feature of our governments. The theory is that all that can should be done by the local authority, and that public expenditure should be chiefly controlled by those who contribute to it.[36]

'Non-partisanship' was an ideal aspired to by many involved in

Victorian and Edwardian city politics who sought, in the face of obviously increasing centralisation, to maintain the autonomy of local government and specifically to resist being drawn into the ideological battles of the national political parties. The 'real' government of the towns, it was said, should take place only in the town hall and should consist basically of balancing the accounts and seeing that extravagances were avoided. Such a vision of local government with its frequently expressed distaste for the meddling of Westminster in what it was claimed were purely local matters, appealed to the small-business owners, most of whom, after all, were largely dependent on local markets for their supplies and sales. Thus, petit-bourgeois forces in the towns and cities up and down the country wove together a normative conception of local government in which 'economy', 'localism', and 'non-partisanship' were closely threaded together. And they used this to 'legitimate' their periodic domination of local administrations. The big-business owners were interested in large, costly schemes; they ran large enterprises and were increasingly oriented to national and international markets and national parties. The local, small-business operators were, so they claimed, the best guardians of *local* government.

In order to press their claims and win seats on the city councils, the petite-bourgeoisie frequently sought to mobilize working-class votes by portraying their candidates as representatives of proletarian interests. Like other contenders for power before them, their challenges to more-established groups led to attempts to capture the support of subordinate classes and strata. In many towns the strategy worked, leading to the ousting of bigger-business interests and their replacement by the 'shopocracy'. Throughout the latter half of the nineteenth century, urban politics took the form less of an inter-class struggle – bourgeois against proletarian – than a series of *intra*-class conflicts with control of the urban centres passing to and fro between different elements of the propertied class. In some towns the power of the local small-business interests became thoroughly entrenched. The bigger bourgeois retreated. Their interests, better and better served by the state, meant that national politics became the more important arena for the defence of their concerns with national and indeed, international markets. Today, few towns are run by big-business owners (which is not to deny their influence on local economies and polities).

In some places the power of petit-bourgeois groups has been

maintained right down to the present day and the legitimatory motifs of this stratum remain stamped upon their political cultures. In Edinburgh, for instance, the so-called 'Progressive Association' consisting chiefly of local, small-business owners held power from the 1920s until the eve of the reorganisation of local government in the 1970s. In 1973, the year in which many defected to the Tory party, the Progressive manifesto proclaimed the original creed:

> Progressives stand for local government by local people, whose duty is to the ratepayers of Edinburgh alone, and not to any national political party. We see good government of the city as an end in itself.[37]

But Edinburgh is hardly typical. In many of our larger and more industrial centres, the small-business elements were challenged. The initial alliance between this stratum and the working class proved fragile. Increasingly, workers organized themselves to confront the small employers and the small-property holders who were their bosses and their landlords. In the late nineteenth century we can see the rise of a 'labour' interest in the town halls. To petit-bourgeois city fathers, such a movement was threatening and illegitimate in that very frequently it sought to locate local struggles in a wider conflict, to relate them to national class antagonisms. It was denounced as breaking the moral conventions of local affairs, accused of ending an era of 'good administration' by 'bringing politics into local government'.[38] Organized labour became first an opposition and later the preponderant force in a few British towns. Everywhere it acquired some political voice.

The rise of organized labour

The political arrival of labour marked a further stage in the emergence of the modern city. The working class had been a force to be reckoned with long before it was enfranchised. As we have seen, other classes and strata had appealed for its moral and social support, by mobilizing its considerable presence in the streets. While popular riots were no longer as frequent, street violence was a weapon used with considerable success, often by populists of the right, to manipulate 'public opinion'.

Until the late nineteenth century, however, the interests of the working class were poorly represented. In the early struggles over the incorporation of cities, workers might be invited to join middle-class Radicals and Dissenters in their agitations. The Philosophic Radicals established links between workers and those tradesmen and professionals Neale[39] calls the 'middling classes'. In the early phases of its formation it did not seem implausible to argue that artisans and shopkeepers were close enough to the working class to understand the plight of its members and present its claims.

But alliances between petit-bourgeois elements and the manual workers could not survive the development of a division of labour and an organisation of life both in work and in the community which, by the latter part of the century, had created an obvious material and cultural gulf. Workers began to organize themselves around their own distinctive interests. In the 1870s and 1880s they sought to impress these on 'radical' and sympathetic Liberals and a little later to win electoral contests with their own candidates.[40] Initially 'working-class' interests were often defined in very narrow ways. It was not the struggle of a national or international working class that was being represented but the very particular concerns of small groups. Thus, in Leeds, Birmingham and Wolverhampton, as Hennock[41] points out, 'Labour' first came into politics simply to represent the interests of the council's municipal workers. Trades union leaders, if they had a seat on the council, could defend their members from inside the 'employers' board room'. Thus, some of the earliest working-class activity in politics was concerned with the council not so much as a political institution but as an *employer*.

In most cities the first Labour councillors appeared in the closing decades of the nineteenth century or in the early years of this century. In Edinburgh with its small working class, the first Labour councillor was elected in 1909 for the 'industrial suburb' of Dalry, followed two years later by two more, and by 1913, there were six Labour councillors. The years immediately before and after the war saw the defeat of all six. By 1935 the support for Labour was considerable but despite collecting 25,965 votes compared with the 35,535 which had gone to the new anti-socialist Progressive Association, Labour won only sixteen seats: the Progressives had fifty. Elsewhere the advance of Labour was more substantial. In Glasgow, Labour took control of the city in 1933 and since the 1930s, most British cities have experienced periods, often very long periods, of domination by the Labour Party. In Liverpool, however, Labour took political control only as recently as 1955.[42]

While it is true that the initial involvement of Labour in local political processes was often triggered by strictly local events and conditions, there is no doubt that the growth of organized labour as a major political force during the inter war years owes much to the politicisation of one crucial issue, a national issue – housing. Even by the end of the nineteenth century there had been important changes in the state's treatment of housing. Housing legislation became less permissive, more directive. It went

> from a reiteration of the autonomy of local government to an emphasis on the coercive and executive powers of municipal and national governments, and from an emphasis upon the rights of municipal government to cleanse and demolish houses dangerous to health to an acknowledgement of the municipal authorities' right to become both builder and landlord. By the 1880s parliament had somewhat unconsciously advanced to the stage where the desirability of subsidised municipal housing in urban rental schemes was frankly recognised.[43]

But local authorities generally dragged their feet. There were precious few homes fit for the heroes to come back to in 1919. From that time on housing was never far from the centre of the political struggles in towns and cities. Between 1919 and 1938 there were no fewer than eleven Housing Acts. Housing became a major issue in local elections since it affected so directly both the working class and the property and building interests which were frequently heavily represented on the town councils. Landlords, already caught by the restrictions of the 1915 Act, saw themselves threatened by the prospect of a growing supply of council houses and local builders feared the plans to use direct labour. The Labour Party increasingly presented itself as the champion of the poor and poorly housed and pressed for the fullest use of the municipal powers for slum clearance and the building of council houses. The interests of property grouped themselves under various right-wing banners to 'protect' the citizenry from unwanted expenditure in such programmes.

The emergence of organized labour as a powerful political force was accelerated by the 1928 Local Government Act which gave local authorities responsibility for education, abolished parochial Boards and set up Public Assistance. These measures, alongside the housing and physical planning legislation considerably expanded the role of local government and gave the Labour Party an incentive to strive for political supremacy in the cities.

As with other classes and strata before them, the organized workers brought with them a critique of the old regime, an image of a more desirable social order and a rhetoric with which to legitimate their bid for power. Thus, the allocation of resources was no longer to be left to the market mechanism but would be determined on the basis of need. Housing developments would be geared to need, not profit, and in order to make allocations to families and individuals it would be necessary to arrive at social definitions of need and to create the administrative machinery for the assessment of people and the disposition of resources. Organized labour sought the extension of democracy; the extension of equal treatment politically, socially and legally to all citizens. It sought 'social justice' for the working class in the form of a more equitable division of basic resources in housing, education and health. Both the extension of the rights of citizenship and the partial circumvention of the market as an allocator of goods and services, demanded new machinery for impartial judgement of need and for the management of the expanding stock of public goods.

Precisely as Weber argued, the growth of mass democracy stimulated the growth of bureaucracy. In Glasgow, a city which for 200 years has experienced the most acute housing problems and has tried most deliberately to solve them through public provision, the quest for 'social justice', in terms of this resource, has produced a housing department which Checkland describes as 'a kind of local Leviathan'. In 1975 it 'owned' and managed 158,000 out of Glasgow's 275,000 houses – 57 per cent of the housing stock. Checkland claims that

> Whereas before 1914 the Corporation was seen as a joint-stock company run by the middle classes, since 1933 it as been increasingly a social service run by the Labour Party, centred upon public-sector housing at low rents.[44]

That is certainly contestable on several grounds, but it does express one interpretation of the very marked change which has occurred in that city since its public political life ceased to be dominated by the bourgeoisie.

Cities which have experienced long periods of political control by the Labour Party may have larger housing departments, more extensive welfare services, and generally favour public over private provision but the basic framework of municipal responsibility has been centrally directed, so that even urban centres where organized labour has hardly ever held power, now provide education, welfare, recreation and housing resources. Everywhere this has meant the expansion of administrative, technical and professional jobs in the several bureaucratic agencies directed by the municipal authorities. The growth here of a bureaucratised 'service' stratum is one part of a much broader change in the occupational and social structure, but at this local level it is often easy to see that there exists a tension between the elected representatives and the salaried officials. Local government has moved from rule by a narrow patriciate to its more open modern form. It has become more democratic. But that democratic system of rule is precarious. It is constantly under threat from two directions: from privileged, propertied groups who seek to return power to the hands of business owners, especially those who stand to gain most from urban growth and property development, and from the rising stratum of officials who aspire to some form of bureaucratic domination.

Conclusion

In this chapter, we have explored the emergence of the modern city through the medium of political change. In this way we can see how politics became a vehicle whereby different class interests expressed their domination. But it is more complicated than that.

Throughout most of the nineteenth century, local politics were fought out not between bourgeois and proletarian, but between different groups *within* the middle class. Sometimes the confrontations were between large- and small-business owners, but frequently they were more complex. The middle class was growing and becoming more differentiated as new jobs appeared: clerical jobs and managerial ones, jobs in public administration, in education and in expanding trade and commercial occupations.

Status distinctions were made, sustained and elaborated. The physical shape of the late Victorian town with its rapidly expanding and internally homogeneous suburbs, with its plethora of churches and meeting halls, recorded the diversity of the growing class of those who were neither proletarian nor properly bourgeois. And local politics provided an arena for many of the status struggles; not only were there Dissenters against Anglicans, but fundamentalists and evangelical groups of various kinds confronted those belonging to more established denominations and Temperance Associations squared up to the representatives of the drink trade. Only rarely were class interests expressed in a simple and direct way.

By looking at cities and towns as 'moments in a process of usurpation and defence, consolidation, appropriation and resistance; as battles rather than as monuments',[45] we can follow Weber's strictures that we should be more interested in the underlying processes of struggle. In looking at the physical form of modern cities, we can see the residues left by earlier battles and victories: at the guild halls, the town halls, the churches and the factories.

But the process is not complete. New forms of political control and cultural domination are expressed in the public housing estates, the modern civic centres, and town precincts, the towers and office blocks reflecting new sets of economic, social and political forces. In the next two chapters, we will explore the parts played by new sets of contestants in this game of urban chess: the bureaucrats and the property men.

Chapter 4

Bureaucracy, Politics and the City

In the last thirty years or so local authorities, especially the big urban authorities, have been obliged to assume greatly extended responsibilities over many aspects of the collective life of their citizens. Housing, welfare, education, local economic development, physical planning – all these and many other issues are now matters of direct concern to the politicians and officials who make up local administrations. In order to carry out their commitments and meet both the demands of central government and the aspirations of their constituents, local politicians have had to allow or encourage the growth of large bureaucratic departments to deal with housing, highways, social services and the like. These bureaucratic structures with their rational organisation, hierarchy of offices and concern with procedure and universalistic rules have become the means whereby an increasingly large stock of public goods is distributed.

Expenditure by local authorities on real resources has risen sharply. Whereas in 1955 this expenditure represented 8.5 per cent of Gross Domestic Product, in 1975 it had risen to 14.5 per cent.[1] Dunleavy has shown that between 1955 and 1975:

> Current expenditure on goods and services increased by nearly 250 per cent, while grants and subsidies administered or provided by local authorities increased by over 550 per cent. The most rapidly growing areas were the personal social services, education, grants for higher education, housing subsidies paid as rent rebates, and support for urban public transport services . . . Overall, local government expenditure in 1975 was three times larger than in 1955.[2]

This growth in expenditure in real terms has been translated into expanded employment opportunities in the local authority sector.[3] Between 1961 and 1979, there was a spectacular 63 per cent increase in the number employed by local authorities, and 54 per cent in the civilian civil service, compared with a decrease of 5 per cent in both the private sector and in public corporations. Local authorities now employ over three million people, some 12.5 per cent of those in work.

The growth of bureaucratically organized, allocative structures has been noted by many urban sociologists but surprisingly little extended discussion can be found and few empirical studies have been made of the actual day-to-day workings of these public bureaucracies. For the most part, urban sociologists have not paid much attention to the implications of bureaucratic development for local politics and few writers have sought to put this growth of bureaucracy into a broad historical perspective. Yet both are needed. Thus, in this chapter we shall try to argue:

- That we are witnessing an extension of bureaucratic domination in local government. This is not to assert that everywhere the 'office holders' have usurped the power of elected representatives, but it is to claim that this happened in some cities and that it may occur in most. The relative positions of politicians and bureaucrats vary from place to place but nowhere is the domination of the office holder unequivocally legitimated.
- That bureaucratic authorities not only affect the life chances of citizens by the granting or withholding of access to housing, open space and recreational resources but that they have increasingly powerful voices in the distribution of jobs, as employers in their own right, as licencees and as the providers of contracts.
- That there is a moral dimension to the growth of bureaucratic authority which sustains and amplifies the 'moral servitude' of the working class already created by the economic and political superiority of the bourgeoisie.

The nature of bureaucratic power

In his analysis of the development of the modern state, Weber saw very clearly the uneasy relationship which exists between democracy and bureaucracy. Democracy, in common with other forms of political domination, needs administration. Nevertheless, says Weber,[4]

Democracy as such is opposed to the 'rule' of bureaucracy, in spite of, and perhaps because of its unavoidable yet unintended promotion of bureaucratization.

He warns us explicitly of the dangers which attend the growth of bureaucratization for while this mode of organization may be required by the scale and complexity of contemporary institutions and may be positively encouraged by the attempts to create a more just and equitable society, it may also come to exert illegitimate power. There is a real prospect that those who occupy bureaucratic offices may usurp the authority of elected representatives, be they members of Parliament or local councillors, and establish a new form of rule in which the principal legitimating device is the claim to expertise.

For Weber, a major problem confronting the advanced nations was the control of these bureaucratic tendencies. What he hoped for was the recognition of the specifically political character of much decision-making and reassertion of political power to prevent administrative domination.[5] This was necessary because of the apparent in-built tendency of bureaucracy to exceed its purely instrumental powers. As Burns has put it:

Government through appointed officials becomes, in practice, government by officials.The rationality, skills and experience which are presumed to make officials effective instruments of government can equally make them effective advocates for the preservation and extension of the powers they have.[6]

To Weber, then, control over the means of administration is as important as control over the means of production, particularly as bringing the latter under public ownership will only accentuate bureaucratic domination. For Weber, rationalization and bureaucratization are the core features of modern societies.

It has become almost commonplace now to argue that in Britain the power of the civil service at the national level, and local officials at the municipal level, is such that the politicians are involved not in making policy but merely in implementing schemes initiated by their established and expert 'servants'. At the level of particular cities or regions, this is surely the view behind Ray Pahl's 'urban managerialism' where the domination of the 'urban manager' over the politician is assumed but never argued.[7] In his later work, he is at pains to point out that this term should refer more to the middle and upper echelons of local government officers rather than the 'face-to-face' bureaucrat encountered by the client. Certainly the terms 'urban manager' and 'bureaucrat' have to be specified more clearly. A distinction has to be made between the decision-making bureaucrat, the higher official, on the one hand, and the more visible 'street-level' bureaucrat on the counter or at the door. The citizen is transformed into a 'client' largely at the hands of the street-level bureaucrat who has to match the relevant characteristics of the citizen to the eligibility rules of the bureaucracy. While the term 'bureaucrat' will be used here in the main to refer to the higher-level bureaucrat, those near the levers of power, the discretionary power of the lower-level bureaucrat, cannot be forgotten.[8] Indeed, by being in the 'front line', the lower-level bureaucrat performs important functions for the bureaucracy as a whole. As Prottas says:

> By categorising citizens, the street-level bureaucrat 'conventionalizes' their characteristics for the agency. This is a precondition for bureaucratic processing. It is also the first step in the processing, and as such constrains and influences all later steps. In this way the street-level bureaucrat contains contingencies that are important to clients. This is the kernel from which the bureaucrat's power grows.[9]

In much of Pahl's work the bureaucratic allocation of resources is a central theme but despite calling for a comparative analysis of city development, there is no real discussion of urban politics in his writing. Urban managers – by which he generally means officials of local government – are discussed with little reference to those in central government or to their continuous struggles with the local councillors. Thus, the recognition of the importance of bureaucratization is not accompanied by any analysis of urban politics nor by any attempt to relate it explicitly to Weber's writing.

In arguing that there has been an extension of bureaucratic domination over elected representatives, it is necessary to be more explicit about the relationship between the economic and political dimensions of power. Might it not be the case that the question as to who has power over local administration is a relatively unimportant one, that 'real' power rests in the hands of private capital? Weber did not deny that it was possible, and indeed likely in capitalist society, that the interests of capital could be observed behind the political stage, but he was unwilling simply to make this an act of faith, an *a priori* assumption. In theoretical terms, the 'economic' and 'political' dimensions of power were to be treated as analytically separate.

Certainly, local government has become more enmeshed in the economic order. Its increasing dependence on the finance markets and on commercial rates has probably made it more reliant on private capital. Nevertheless, the size and scale of local government has made it a significant actor in the corporate economy. It has become a major customer (for the construction industry, for example); it is directly involved in the financial markets (as owners of pension funds); it collaborates with property capital in land development.

Recent writers on urban politics have shown themselves to be unwilling to accept a narrow economic determinism. Patrick Dunleavy, while accepting the main elements of a neo-Marxist perspective, states, 'I am highly sceptical of any attempt to deduce explanations of urban politics from the structural features of the capitalist mode of production.'[10] Similarly, in his review of the reorganization of local government in Britain, John Dearlove concludes:

It must be recognized that political and governmental processes themselves possess a certain 'internal dynamic' which serves to place them beyond easy 'control' once set in motion almost regardless of either the state of struggle or the functional needs of capital.[11]

The political sphere, including local government, must of course be seen in the wider context of the political economy but is not simply determined by it. In Saunders's opinion, bureaucrats are still left with significant decision-making influence: 'the fact remains that the ecological, political and economic constraints on urban managers serve only to narrow the scope of decision-making; they do not determine it'.[12]

It is within this relative degree of autonomy given to the political sphere that we wish to examine the relationship between local government officials and their political masters.

Bureaucracy in the ascendant?

The belief that officials enjoy considerable power and may well force the elected representatives into subordinate roles is widespread; but on what is it really based? There seem to be several strands of argument. First, there is the claim made by Marxists and non-Marxists alike that local government lacks any real autonomy and is simply the 'field-agent' of the central state. One of the most recent and explicit formulations of this view is provided by Cockburn who argues that 'the council is only a small part of a large state structure'.[13] In her view, the role of the state is 'to keep the working class in its place and to set things up with forceful sanctions, in such a way that capital itself, business interests as a whole, normally survive and prosper'.[14] And Lambeth council, the subject of her study, is a part of that project since it represents the state locally: it is the 'local state'. From this perspective there is no doubt about the weakness of the local politicians for it is alleged, whenever they show any socialist zeal, they are overruled by the officials. Local government provides the arena in which the forces of civil society and the state confront each other. It is the mechanism through which most state-provided services are delivered, and it plays a most important part in the reproduction of capitalist relations.

A good many non-Marxists go along with much of this argument. Thus Michael Hill observes:

> One of the salient features of British local government is enshrined in the doctrines of 'ultra vires' which prevents local authorities doing anything they have not got Parliamentary permission to do. Moreover, a great deal of legislation that affects local government is *mandatory* rather than permissive, and central government also has a great deal of control over local authority finance, so that, all in all, most local government work involves the implementation of central government legislation. All this suggests that it is appropriate to categorise local government as 'administration'.[15]

However, he goes on to claim that this characterisation is too simple, and to show the considerable variations that can exist in the styles of local government. Not all of them can be dismissed in this way. Councillors can act in ways which make it essential to distinquish 'politics' from administration and there are circumstances under which the power of the bureaucrats cannot be assumed to be dominant. None the less, it is hard to deny that the *trend* has been towards greater and greater subordination of local government to the central authority and to the major bureaucracies of Whitehall. In these circumstances, the influence of local politicians has waned and that of the full-time officials, especially the senior ones, has grown.

A second argument for the subordination of local politics to bureaucratic administration and to the central state is found if one looks at local electoral behaviour. It seems that success or failure depends more on the popularity of the party in power at Westminster than on the virtues or deficiencies of local administrations and local parties.[16] Votes are cast to express a judgement of central government rather than to applaud or censure the local councillors. Under these circumstances, the municipal officers who watch the elected representatives come and go in so haphazard a fashion acquire the legitimacy of experience and durability.

Third, local bureaucrats, particularly those at the top of specialized departments such as planning, architecture, public health, education and social work are *professionals* with 'expertise' and with allegiances to professional associations.[17] Their esoteric knowledge legitimates their authority: they are experts whose very special skills are symbolized in titles and degrees and impenetrable jargon. Loyalty to professional associations with their standards both practical and ethical, encourage many to claim a degree of autonomy from the demands of their political masters and also from other groups of bureaucrats. Professional identities provide a rich source of rivalry within local government and despite attempts to create more unified and cohesive bureaucratic structures in local government, departmental jealousies are still very evident.[18] The part-time amateur councillors are increasingly faced with permanent officers whose expertise is daunting. Heclo, in his study of Manchester councillors, encountered a Conservative businessman who told him that 'policy and administration have actually been reversed. The officer formulates the policy and the committee argues about the technicalities of administering it.' And a Labour member who observed:

My committee can do little more than rubber stamp things . . .
Even when an officer comes to us for instructions, the committee is
baffled. We have to ask him, 'well, what did you have in mind?'.
We're more than guided, we're directed.[19]

Similar reports can be found in other studies. Evidence for administrative domination based on and legitimated by 'expertise' is widespread and Hill, in constructing three models of local government, labels this form 'administrative politics'.[20] Politicians are circumvented, their lack of technical knowledge rendering their judgements irrelevant or unsound as far as the professionally trained bureaucrat is concerned. In some authorities, it is alleged, the councillors carry out routine administrative tasks – like vetting the expense claims of their officials – while the latter get on with the serious business of designing real policies and engaging in 'real' politics. In some circumstances, the officials go over the heads of the councillors and bargain directly with pressure groups and local interests, undermining the authority of the politician in his ward by establishing direct lines of communication with those affected by, say, a planning decision. Sometimes, by insisting on formalized and universal procedures to meet a public demand, the bureaucrats destroy the 'patronage' dispensed by local politicians and weaken still further the traditional authority of the democratically elected representatives.

R. J. Buxton, who was once a Labour councillor himself, certainly offers support for this view of local politics. The councillors, he stresses, are strictly 'amateurs' and local government is now, in his opinion, far too complex to be left to them:

Nothing seems more obvious than that a larger role will have to be played in the future by full-time professionals who have the knowledge and the time to cope with the complexities of modern life, let alone of modern government. Local government's present arrangements for controlling those professionals are undemocratic precisely because they are totally unrealistic. The officials in theory have no power, whilst in fact they control almost everything that happens, either from Town Hall or Whitehall.[21]

And one of the sources of that power is found in the officials' role as the mediators between national and local administrations for they have 'professional' links to the bureaucrats in Whitehall. Given the legal status of the local corporation, with its limited spheres of competence, their interpretation of legislation and of advice and guidance from the Ministries is crucially important. The sharing of technical competences and social networks with their counterparts in the central bureaucracies is yet one more way in which the power of the local official is maintained.

The trend toward bureaucratic domination is not equally well established in all local authorities but it should not be thought that it occurs only in those where 'political' authority has been weakened by frequent changes of political personnel or those with mainly working-class representatives. Lee, in his study of county government in Cheshire, shows how some officials become social leaders and how the status of politicians can become, in a way, dependent on their relationships with the bureaucratic 'notables'. The county had seen the replacement of its traditional social leaders by 'a community of public persons in which the leading members and the chief officers of the county council were the principal personalities'. And he goes on to spell out the relationship between the two more clearly:

> the leading councillors were those who learned to acquire the art of understanding discussions at 'officer level' and who thereby gained the confidence of the chief officers. Such men, if they were also respected by the organisations of the political parties, and had the necessary ability to grasp the intricacies of the administrative detail involved, constituted an informal group of 'ministers', the 'inner ring'. They, in alliance with the chief officers constituted a kind of ministerial party, grouped around the persons of the chairman and vice-chairman of the council . . . promotion into the 'inner ring' depended upon making an impression upon not only one's immediate colleagues but also upon the chief officers and chairmen.[22]

All this in the relatively unpromising setting of a Conservative county council.

The advantages enjoyed by senior local government officials over their political masters are then considerable: they include the general prestige of professional training, the more specific social honour dependent upon the officials' relationships with other powerful bureaucrats or with economic and social notables in the district as well as the technical skills, the support of a professional association and the administrative and research resources they command. The bureaucratization of local government grows as the range of public services expands. The more local government is expected to be an efficient provider of services – like education, housing, transport – the less it conforms with Sharpe's[23] other two 'values' of local government – as an aid to democracy and to public participation in government. As local government becomes more and more a matter of 'administration' rather than 'politics' so its democratic features recede. It is not possible to construct any simple generalizations about the extent of bureaucratic power in British local authorities but the historic drift is plain enough. As Cox concludes:

> We have seen the emergence into a dominating role of the official, the professional basing his claim to a place in the policy-making sun not on representativeness but on expertise. He and the politician now rule as a duumvirate, the balance between the two being variable from service to service and from town to town.[24]

Bureaucratic power constrained

Does this mean that we should take a pessimistic view of future developments, seeing only the progressive attrition of democracy and the uncheckable advance of bureaucratic domination? In our view – no. While they may not provide grounds for wild optimism, there are certain developments which encourage us to believe that local government could be made more amenable to democratic scrutiny and control; that new forms of participatory democracy are possible.

One encouraging sign is the extent of public unrest[25] at many official decisions. This seems to be growing rather than receding as more and more citizens – not only the middle class – are prepared to challenge bureaucratic decisions which affect their lives. Opposition to city motorway schemes, resistance to plans for comprehensive redevelopment or to destructive forms of urban 'renewal' has been seen on occasion to succeed, stopping the planners and road engineers from implementing plans with serious social consequences. The much vaunted 'expertise' of the planners and architects has been shown, in many instances, to be little more than a blind for what are highly subjective decisions. Though they have lost far more battles than they have won, working-class people, whether tenants of the corporation or private landlords or owners of small cottages or 'semis', have seen through the esoteric language of council officials, have seen how spurious are many of the supposedly expert and technically sophisticated arguments. Writers like Norman Dennis[26] and Jon Davies[27] have exploded many of the comforting myths about the public sensitivity and openness of public authority officials, Social workers, political activists and others[28] have revealed how much 'participation' is a sham and the effect of all this is to build a great scepticism about official decision-making, and about forms of public enquiry and a heightened awareness that the citizenry is not entirely impotent. Community action groups, tenants' associations and the like have demonstrated that organized protest can succeed. It is hard to see in these ephemeral groupings with their generally very restricted objectives and a-political character the 'urban social movements' of which Castells and others write, but there is no doubt that there is a growing resentment of the extensiveness and seeming insensitivity of bureaucratic power.

A second trend which promises to counter the power of officialdom is the tendency for local government to become more strictly organized along party lines and for many more issues to be 'politicized'. Steadily, particularly in the cities, the old tradition of 'non-partisan' politics has diminished. Young's study of local government in London[29] is the best account of this process but it has been occurring very widely. The 1960s saw the demise of many of the non-political groups – the Moderates, Progressives and Independents – and their replacement by official Conservative candidates. This ties local politics more firmly to national politics but at the same time, it strengthens the 'politicians' against the bureaucrats. As we learned in our study of councillors in Edinburgh,[30] the collapse of the local 'non-partisan' Progressive Association came about in large part because many with right-wing sympathies felt that the local business people who made up that body are mostly incapable of dealing with the 'expert' officials. They saw the possibility under the Tory banner of promoting a new breed of councillor, younger and more highly educated, able to confront the bureaucrats and able too to call upon the expertise and resources of a national party for information and guidance.

The bureaucratisation of local government is constantly developing new organizational forms, for as the scale of activities increases, the problems of co-ordination become more acute. Thus, we find in recent years attempts to restructure the administrative apparatus by creating 'chief executives', 'city managers' and forms of 'corporate management' intended to overcome the departmental divisions and jealousies. The effect of this could be greatly to increase the power of the bureaucrats, but in practice, it is often very difficult to break down departmental boundaries and 'corporate management' remains an ideal rather than a reality.

In his study of local government reorganisation in Britain, Dearlove believes that not much has in fact changed: 'To a considerable extent . . . we are dealing with familiar old wine that has recently been decanted into strong new misty bottles that are now blessed with modern new technocratic labels.'[31]

The local politicians are not blind to the threats which are posed to their already limited authority. They too alter the traditional ways of doing things. Electoral competition becomes more and more a contest between 'teams' offering varieties of 'sound government' and once in power, the old multi-party committees shrink in favour of single-party 'cabinets' attempting to co-ordinate and direct policy in several committees. Distinctly 'political' attitudes are struck regarding housing, education or social welfare provision. Such a tendency generally weakens the position of the local bureaucrats for markedly divergent policies make it difficult to maintain a consistent pattern of administration. A bipartisan (or non-partisan) approach to, say, housing problems eases the housing manager's task; the sudden call for a radically different policy will lead him or her to 'play politics' with the chairman of committees and leaders of the dominant party in order to minimize disruption to his or her own preferred programme. Thus, politicisation and bureaucratisation may be developing side by side, changes in one calling out responses in the other as politicians and bureaucrats jockey for control of public resources.

This leads to the view that we may need another 'model' for local government. Not all challenges have led toward 'administrative politics' and Hill proposes that we should refer to government by party machines as 'ideological politics'. Where distinct parties compete with different programmes, we find that once elected, they 'distribute patronage on party lines, and will present to the administrators certain general objectives or policies with which they expect specific measures to be compatible'.[32] The role of the adminstrator is more constrained because more issues are defined as 'political', and less as merely 'administrative'. Thus the allocation of public housing is the subject of party policy rather than of officialdom.

Bureaucratic power in local authorities in Britain is also likely to be constrained by the capacity of the political parties to orchestrate and absorb the protest activities of groups of citizens. The class-based parties in most instances succeed in encapsulating issues and whenever there is a threat that they might escape the boundaries of party, efforts are made to bring the pressure groups – ratepayers' associations, tenants' organisations, community action groups – under the party umbrellas. And this is facilitated by the fact that in Britain local government is relatively formalized and tightly structured so that it is difficult for protest or interest groups to bargain directly with officials or with political figures representing separate local authority bodies. The British system is unlike that in the USA,[33] where there is a great deal of formal decentralisation with many separate authorities to be played off one against another. The American system offers a great deal of scope for bargaining and local bureaucrats are frequently drawn in to act as 'brokers', a fact which gives them a good deal of power. In Britain more unified formal structures, together with the considerable degree of central governmental control make it harder for the bureaucrats to engage in 'bargaining' politics and easier for the major parties to channel the pressures of diverse groups.

The local and national state

The enormously increased intervention of the state in the economic and social life of the country over the past thirty years or so has meant that local authorities have been called upon to expand vastly the area of their responsibility for the welfare of citizens. In many ways the growth of state power has eroded that autonomy of which Victorian city fathers were so proud. There is no disputing the extent of central governmental financial involvement: wheras in 1891, just over half of local government revenue came from central grants, by the 1970s, it was over two-thirds.[34] Dunleavy has calculated that between 1935 and 1975 central government grants to local authority current receipts had risen by over 16 per cent, those from non-domestic (commercial) rates had remained at around a quarter of receipts, whereas domestic rates had fallen back by 12 per cent, providing less than 13 per cent of local authority current revenue.[35]

For many contemporary writers, such figures simply corroborate their view that the financial and legal subordination of local authorities is such that they can be regarded simply as 'agents' of the state. To take this position, though, is to ignore the fact that a good deal of discretionary power is left for local authorities. In his review of local and central government relations, Dearlove concludes: 'There are firm grounds for claiming that local authorities are by no means the passive agents of the central government but have scope to developtheir own policies.'[36]

To date, then, he who has paid the piper around two-thirds of his income – central government – has been reluctant to call at least all the tunes in the repertoire. Certainly, recent governments have sought to restrain local government spending, and no measure has challenged fiscal autonomy more than the Conservative Government's Local Government Act of 1980,[37] much to the alarm of its local government allies.[38]

Nevertheless, considerable discretionary power remains. The many services which city and regional governments are called upon to provide, the vast resources which they control, may be allocated in various ways and it is exactly around this issue of allocative power that much local politics is fought out. Educational policies can vary considerably from one authority to another and fourteen years after the central government called for the establishment of comprehensive schooling in England and Wales there are still a few authorities defying Westminster. Transport provision, general physical planning and, above all, housing policies, reveal the extent of local discretion. Local politicians and their permanent officials can decide on the level of public housing provision, on the 'mix' of tenures, the location of council housing schemes, the kind of welfare and other services provided in these areas and the allocation of tenants to the various housing schemes.

There is no sense in exaggerating the capacity of local authorities to evade the wishes of central government but education, housing and social service provisions all indicate clearly enough the way that Westminster often shrinks from too open a conflict with the local bodies. The reasons for this are not too hard to find. There is the history of local autonomy to contend with. The extent of municipal freedom has always been exaggerated but even as a 'myth' it is important and all the major parties – Labour as much as the Tories – sustain it. Left-wing governments in Britain have never argued against the idea that democracy requires strong local government. Thus, despite glaring inequalities, as for instance between inner London boroughs like Lambeth and an area like Surrey, central government has generally been timid about intervention. As Young and Kramer[39] have shown, the suburban authorities have very successfully headed off attempts to persuade them to help alleviate the problems of inner-city decay and overcrowding. They have done so in part because the notion of local autonomy is so deeply embedded in the general conception of democratic politics in Britain.

The persistence of the belief in autonomy[40] coupled with the great expansion of publicly provided services has meant that in many ways the lives of individuals and families are now more dependent upon decisions made by the bureaucrats and councillors than ever before. None of us is unaffected by the patterns of revenue raising, expenditure or control dictated by the town hall. There has been created an enormous public property and control of this is an extremely significant form of power in contemporary society. Control of the agencies which allocate public funds and resources confers power both over 'collective consumption' and over some elements of production. Local authorities use many devices to lure industrial enterprises and offices to their local sites and factories; they try by various means to generate or sustain small businesses and they have authority to licence certain trades or control their location.

Accepting that there are some developments which partially counterbalance the influence of the 'expert' official in local government, the scale and complexity of this public property none the less makes it difficult for most 'amateur' politicians to oversee. Access to the 'new property',[41] consisting of rights to basic resources like housing or health care or education or even the right to pursue a particular business is increasingly in the hands of local bureaucrats. In industrial sociology, there has been much discussion of the power of the bureaucrats in private enterprise but despite pleas from writers like Ray Pahl there is much less interest in the role of those who administer public resources. Perhaps this is in part because the general conception of these actors and of the institutions in which they work has been too narrow. We need to place the growth of these public bureaucracies in a longer historical perspective and see the very rapid and very large growth of employment in local authority agencies and the money and resources commanded by them as one part of the general development of an economy and a polity in which public property now plays a major role.

Command over the means of administering this public property is in theory in the hands of democratically elected representatives, but in practice their grip on the machinery of administration is far from firm. Thus, those who on a day-to-day basis run the agencies – the housing departments, the social services departments – are very often the real controllers. Moreover, their power is enhanced by the flourishing of parallel structures of administration in public agencies which operate locally but are not part of the municipal or regional government. Some, like local offices of the Department of Health and Social Security, are answerable to Westminster but others, like development agencies, are for most practical purposes outside any popular democratic control There is no doubt that much that a local authority may wish to do bears on the operation of these other bureaucratic agencies and close relationships between the staff of central, local and quasi-governmental bodies have grown up. There is in effect a bureaucratic nexus, subject to rather limited public scrutiny or control, which commands the vast new property.

In these circumstances, what we need is not simply an understanding of the role of the 'gatekeepers' or 'managers' of the urban system but a thorough-going sociology of public bureaucracy[42] which will recognize the transformations of economy and polity which have attended its growth. What we may be witnessing in local government is the usurpation of political power by the bureaucratic 'middle class', first in the obvious sense of direct control by officials, second, through the diffuse nexus which relates local government officials to state and quasi-governmental agencies and third, through the emergence of members of the bureaucratic middle class as councillors themselves.

The extension of bureaucratic power

In his discussion of power in the medieval city, Weber described, as Spencer[43] has recently reminded us, the ways in which formal, legitimate power is extended so as to become informal, illegitimate and diffuse. That is precisely what has happend with the growth of bureaucratic power in local authorities in Britain. Take, for instance, the power which planners exercise. Behind their schemes for urban renewal or suburban development there are statutory powers and statutory responsibilities, but it is obvious that because any sizeable programme of urban change will affect surrounding areas, those who plan the new schemes exercise a diffuse influence over far more than the acres represented on their drawing boards. Their decisions reverberate through the domestic and work lives of many more than those they are authorized to assist or compensate. In addition, many of the larger schemes for central-city areas involve other public bureaucracies in what becomes a joint venture between, say, the corporation, a university or a health board or a civil service department and one or more private developers. The effect of large-scale operations of this kind is to give a good deal of power to bureaucrats who are in no direct way accountable to those whose lives may be affected. A university or some other public body may be allowed or even encouraged over a period of many years to buy up residential and commercial property in an area slated for comprehensive redevelopment. It is not clear to whom its 'officers' are really accountable. Not usually to any general assembly of those who work and study in it and certainly not to the residents of the area over which it extends its influence. People's lives and livelihoods are directly affected by these bureaucratic combinations but they often lack the institutionalized means of calling them to account. The growth of bureaucratic power has outstripped the development of democratic checks and where several bureaucracies collaborate, it is not easy to establish responsibility or find ways of reasserting political control.

But it is in the development and management of public housing that we see most clearly the extension and diffusion of bureaucratic power. In all major cities housing is the most pressing problem and many studies reveal how in situations of great need and scarcity even the 'first-line bureaucrats' – the men and women behind the counters in the housing department – acquire the capacity to affect the life chances of a family in a fundamental way. Out of the myriad day-to-day decisions concerning applications and allocations, tacit rules develop whereby what are essentially moral judgements can be exercised.[44] In some authorities, formal rules and systems exist for the screening of applicants and their assignment to categories of 'respectability'. The management of housing expands to become an exercise in social control and it is the poorest and weakest sections of the community who are corralled into the least desirable housing areas where lack of work and lack of amenities commonly perpetuate the economic difficulties of those sent there and where the reputation of the area stigmatizes and limits access to opportunities outside its boundaries.[45] It is often the case that discretionary control over access to public goods lies in the hands, not of the top policy-making bureaucrats, but of the lower echelons in the system, the 'street-level bureaucrats', in Lipsky's phrase,[46] who interpret the regulations in order to admit or exclude clients. As Prottas says:

> the street-level bureaucrat attempts to obtain a measure of autonomy in order to pursue his own interests and to retain the flexibility needed to respond to a complex and unpredictable environment . . . As a result, the street-level bureaucrat exercises discretion in the categorisation of clients which is unsanctioned by the organisation for which he works.[47]

In their quest for 'stability' and 'order' and even 'fairness' the housing departments have become prime agents in the control of the working class, not only shifting and sorting more from less 'respectable' but also developing techniques for the management of conflicts (establishing residents' associations with non-resident teachers, ministers and others as members, for example) and able increasingly to call on other bureaucracies for further information about areas and individuals. The growth of bureaucracy has often meant that the same individuals and families appear in records of several bureaux and exchange of information facilitates control of 'problem families'. In the worst instances, the poor are forced into a dependency akin to 'institutionalisation'. The public property has produced new and essentially illegitimate forms of domination on the part of bureaucrats. The concern with material conditions in the city as in the wider society, has not been matched by any comparable concern with any moral needs — with the need for personal dignity.

Finally, we might note the way in which the notion of bureaucratic 'expertise' and the respect for formal training and experience become weapons to be used in confrontations with self-help groups. Departments of social work, for instance, may see grass-roots area organisations as a threat, substituting as they often do 'amateur' for the 'professional' social worker. Jobs, budgets and the means of control are all at stake.

Thus, we are suggesting that we should relate the growth of local government bureaucracy to the rapid expansion of public property. Control over that property conveys material benefits, political power and prestige. Public property has not replaced private productive property but it does stand as a new and extensive source of power over which a constant struggle has developed. It is a struggle with several contestants and there are no inevitable or necessarily durable outcomes. It is a struggle of politicians, both the old bourgeois elements and the established working-class representatives against the expert officials; it is a struggle of a new middle class for control over a potent source of influence; it is a struggle of those who are morally subjugated against the denial of their freedom and their worth.

Chapter 5

Market Forces and Property Relations

Introduction

Social relations in contemporary society cannot be understood without examining property relations. The life chances of individuals, the broad patterns of economic and social inequality, the institutions, culture and ideology in present-day western societies, all reflect fundamental characteristics of the institution of private property and the differential distribution of productive resources.

As they have developed in capitalist systems, property rights refer not simply to the relationships between owners and things: they specify relations between individuals and groups. The right to property is always a right against other people.[1] Thus, property establishes relations of superiority and inferiority, the customs and sentiments that surround it provide many of the most fundamental elements in our social order. Property establishes basic interests and consequently outlines a framework of alliances and oppositions which structure society.

All the classic sociological theorists recognized that diverse forms of property could be found in capitalist economies. Weber observed that property could refer to

> ownership of dwellings, workshops; warehouses, stores; agriculturally usable land in large or small-holdings – a quantitative difference with possible qualitative consequences; ownership of mines; cattle; men (i.e. slaves); disposition over mobile instruments of production, or capital goods of all sorts, especially money or objects that can easily be exchanged for money; disposition over products of one's own labour or of others' labour differing according to their various distances from consumability; disposition over transferable monopolies of any kind – all these distinctions differentiate the class situations of the propertied.[2]

Those forms of property which most commonly attract our attention today are those which are central to our industrial economies; the ownership of industrial plant, raw materials, commercial resources and the stocks and shares and money invested in manufacture and trade. It is these that do most to shape the class structure and class relations in the world in which we live, and they affect profoundly the character of social life in our cities. But Weber's catalogue alerts us to the fact that aside from these forms of property which mould the character of our labour markets and the world of work, there are others – urban land and real estate and the finances for their development – which affect all of us who live in cities.

In Britain, as in other western countries, the cities have changed a good deal in the past thirty years or so. They have changed physically as old streets and houses have been swept away to be replaced by towers of offices or multi-storey flats and by the suburban spread of private and public housing and new complexes of industry and commerce. They have changed socially as a consequence of migration and patterns of household formation, with new ethnic enclaves being established and sharper patterns of status segregation appearing.[3] The forces underlying these changes are complex, involving secular economic shifts, individual choices of life styles and environment and political decisions. And they have been accomplished through confrontations and compromises reached in the struggles between politicians and bureaucrats and groups of citizens and those who own land or, who develop, build and rent houses, offices and industrial sites.

Weber recognized that urban land, housing and other forms of real estate could be more than just items of consumption. For those who owned or controlled them, they were, and are, real sources of power. Ownership confers rights: rights of exclusion, rights to decide who should or should not have access, rights to revenue and to capital accumulation. Thus, if we try to understand the obvious and visible changes in the spatial and social ordering of the cities, we must begin with property and property relations.

In recent years there have been some broad changes in the patterning of property relations in the city. There has been a decline in the ranks of local entrepreneurs and property holders, of the landlords and their agents, of local builders and property dealers. It is a decline which is part of a general reduction of local and petit-bourgeois elements in our industrial and commercial systems. There has been a corresponding rise in the significance of large enterprises: the big builders, the large property developers and property companies whose activities have become not simply national, but international in scope. And alongside their growth there has occurred the formation and development of financial institutions providing the capital for ever larger projects and using the benefits of urban real estate for private profit and the collective security of their investors. The role of the state both locally and nationally has been vastly extended, facilitating the construction of huge stocks of public housing, altering the rights of property holders, constraining some elements, assisting the growth of others. And everywhere, in Britain, there has been the rapid and politically sponsored spread of home ownership, conferring upon millions of households small but far from insignificant stakes in the system of property rights.

In this chapter, these are the principal changes in property relations we wish to explore.

The local property owners and the world they have lost

One hundred years ago only a small minority of the population of our British cities owned any urban land or real estate. Probably less than 10 per cent of the households owned the flats and houses they lived in. Property, whether in housing, industrial establishments, shops, offices or urban land was in the hands either of traditional 'landed' families or local bourgeois families. By the end of the Second World War a little more than a quarter of the households in Great Britain owned their own homes, about 13 per cent lived in council property and the remaining 60 per cent or so were still in privately rented accommodation. Thus, until very recently, the great bulk of urban housing was in the hands of landlords, most of whom were local bourgeois or petit-bourgeois individuals or families.

In the lives of these people, property had both material and symbolic significance. The ownership of sites or tenements, or rows of cottages could be a source of income and accumulation. In good years, when town building was booming, as in the 1870s, for example, the jobbing builders did very well out of the sale of their houses and so long as demand for their particular kinds of housing was high, so too did the landlords. But there were lean years when builders went bust and periods such as the 1890s when landlords with anything other than the cheapest forms of property had seriously to compete with each other to attract tenants. There were periodic gluts of housing for the middle class and the better-paid elements of the working class.[4] However, all in all, property was viewed throughout the Victorian period as a relatively secure investment though not one which would yield spectacular profits and it was this which induced many local business owners and professionals to put their money, as they said, 'into stone and lime'. In a society without the pension schemes and insurance provisions which we take for granted, property could give security in old age or could be used by and transmitted to dependants. Today, a good many landlords in the much reduced sector of private rental (in 1979 the sector provided about 13 per cent of the dwellings in Britain) are the descendants of those who invested in property many years ago[5] and the residue of those stocks and property left to children, wives, unmarried female kin or other dependants provided in the 1950s and 1960s, the means whereby property entrepreneurs could begin their often lucrative careers.

But there was, and is, more to the ownership of property than material interest. Acquiring property even on a modest scale could represent an avenue of social mobility.[6] It represented a stake in the wider system of property ownership and served, in the context of local status systems, as an indicator of moral and social worth. T. H. Marshall identified the sociological relevance of real estate ownership when he wrote:

> the significance of property in determining social attitudes is enormous, not because of the income it yields, but because it is a guarantee of the right to enjoy the blessings of civilization. It means that we shall not be cast out in the social wilderness, it shows that we are solid and to be trusted to fulfil our obligations, and that we can move freely in the heart of a great society.[7]

Those who did not enjoy the benefits of possession could recognize the reality of the power of property when they confronted the legal backing given to a landlord, defending the latter's right to dispose of his property as he saw fit and in some instances to restrain and have sold off the furniture and personal effects of indebted tenants.[8] And it was visible too if one looked at the composition of many a town council in Victorian and Edwardian Britain.

But if that is the traditional significance, and it still has some force today, many of those who inherited or invested in rented property no longer regard it as quite such a blessing. Rent controls, first implemented in 1915, compulsory purchase, planning restrictions and the growth of public housing have all served to limit the power, and often the profits, of those who hold rented housing. In all sectors of the property market, as elsewhere in our economy, there has been a shift towards larger organisations; bigger builders, specialist development companies, large-scale landlords for domestic and commercial property and massive institutional investors to provide finance. The business of constructing, leasing, buying and selling has largely passed out of the hands of local factors, lawyers and estate agents and large diversified corporations have replaced them. The stratum of local 'property owners' has undergone a real decline and many of the older landlords to whom we spoke in the course of our research, lamented what they saw as the demise of a parochial social order where groups of local bourgeois 'invested in their town' and parlayed their holdings of property into acknowledged claims for prestige and a measure of political power.[9]

Property booms and the developers

Since the last war, in Britain as in most western societies, there have been some remarkable developments in the patterns of property relations in the cities. We have witnessed the growth of what is really a new industry of property holding and property development with the emergence of enormously rich companies undertaking the reconstruction or growth of urban housing, offices and the commercial and industrial fabric. Some commentators see three main phases in this. The first, a building boom in the 1950s and 1960s in which offices, shops and to a lesser degree housing, provided the bases for new or rapidly expanding construction and development firms; the second, a financial boom triggered by the Chancellor of the Exchequer, Anthony Barber, who allowed extraordinary lending powers to banks and other financial institutions and stimulated enormous property speculation; and a third and much more recent boom in factory and warehouse building.[10]

James Lorimer, in his detailed study of the development industry in Canada,[11] suggests that we can see the first two decades after the war constituting what he calls the 'entrepreneurial' phase, and although our British cities have not grown in the dramatic manner of many settlements in North America,[12] his term seems appropriate in describing the character of the initial activity. Several things fueled the original post-war boom. First, there was the need for reconstruction at the end of the war. In London, the blitz had destroyed a major part of the City and dockside areas and industrial sites had been substantially damaged. Coupled with the general neglect during those war years, this meant that in the capital, and in other large centres, there was a desperate need for domestic accommodation and for industrial and commercial rebuilding. Many of the fortunes of the property tycoons grew out of these first attempts at reconstruction. Marriott, in his study of the property boom,[13] describes how men like Charles Clore, Harold Samuel and Joe Levy bought up the ruins and the bomb sites for small sums and then, when the war ended, found themselves with assets whose value escalated rapidly. In the 1950s the changing structure of industry led to a huge demand for office space to house the bureaucratic apparatus of large companies. As the complexity of their operations grew, so too did their need for co-ordinating systems, for access to the means of communication and for proximity to complementary enterprises. The result was enormous pressure for central-city office space. Alongside the private companies, the state's apparatus was growing rapidly too and the civil service and the local authorities themselves required more and more accommodation. The peak of the office-building boom came in the early 1960s, producing massive profits for the developers.

Books by Marriott and Jenkins and reports like that by Counter Information Services,[14] all documented the meteoric rise to fame and fortune enjoyed by a handful of new property entrepreneurs. Probably the most remarkable company engaged in the development of the office-building boom in London was the Stock Conversion group run by Robert Clark and Joe Levy. From an intitial investment of £100 in 1954, the company grew and by 1973 it had over £55 million of assets. Its most notorious development was the Euston Centre. An original one-acre site was acquired by Joe Levy for £400,000 in 1956 after he had obtained planning permission for 120,000 square feet of office space. In a deal with the London County Council who wanted the site for an underpass, Levy was given permission to purchase thirteen acres of adjacent land and to develop *all* of them at the same 120,000 square foot per acre density. Concealing his identity behind three other estate agencies, he bought up all the property on the new site by 1960 and went ahead with the development. The cost of land and building was £16 million, the value on completion £38 million. The Department of the Environment was the tenant for the office space at the initial rent of £1,729,200.

Most of the 'property barons' were essentially self-made men who started with small capital and some knowledge of the estate agents' trade. They had contacts and lots of brash self-confidence. As Marriott observes:

> The developer is a pure entrepreneur. The only equipment he needs is a telephone, and there were powerful developers who operated from their study at home or from a one-roomed office with a secretary. From there they wielded the talents of various professions; estate agents, solicitors, bankers, architects, quantity surveyors, consulting engineers, building contractors, accountants.[15]

The developer's most basic material is land and the art of land assembly was cultivated not only by those who participated in the burgeoning market for office-block development but also by building companies who foresaw the rising demand for suburban housing and attempted to create for themselves sizeable land banks which they could use themselves or gradually sell off to other construction firms. The scale of suburban land assembly has not been as great as that observable in North America, nor has the process been as well researched[16] but there can be little doubt that the fortunes of some construction companies owe much to their owners' skills in establishing almost monopolistic controls over local land markets. The very rapid growth of Miller Construction is a case in point. The late Sir James Miller began with a small building company in Edinburgh, acquired very substantial local land holdings, became Lord Provost of the city and only a few years later, had so extended his activities to the South of England as to warrant his election as Lord Mayor of London, from which lofty position he presided over a large and diversified company involved in all aspects of the property business at home and abroad.

In Lorimer's Canadian study[17] we can see very clearly the importance of land banking, for as local entrepreneurs concentrated land holding in the hands of very few companies, they were able to force up land values and exercise considerable influence over the speed and pattern and profitability of urban growth and reconstruction.

In Britain, the property boom of the 1950s and 1960s though principally based on the speculative development of offices and commercial premises, also benefited from the rapidly rising demand both for home ownership and for rented accommodation. The scale of profits was not so large here and the statutory controls on rents and security of tenure were serious deterrents to would-be speculators, but still some entrepreneurs found ways of exploiting the inflationary rises in property values so as to make their fortunes. Having done very well from their participation in the office developments, the banks and insurance companies and other investors were ready to channel money into domestic property as office construction slowed down. Thus, capital was readily available to entrepreneurs like Stern, when he sought to build up a portfolio of domestic accommodation to complement his commercial holdings. The basic trick was to buy housing, commonly with sitting tenants, for a low price and with a sizeable mortgage. After some while, the existing tenants might be induced to move and new tenants brought in to pay much higher rents on accommodation that had been (in some instances at least) somewhat modernized. On the strength of the higher level of returns, the improvements to the property and the general inflation in house prices, the property could be revalued at considerably more than the intial valuation, thus making it possible for the entrepreneur to obtain more mortgage credit to buy additional property and repeat the process. Stern's Freshwater Properties empire was built up in exactly this way and because he employed close management practices, dealt mainly in fairly substantial middle-class housing and did spend money on renovation, his was described as the 'Marks and Spencer' of property companies.[18] This sobriquet did not, however, prevent the collapse of his company in the wave of failures in 1974.

An alternative strategy was to purchase rented property cheaply and then sell off individual units sometimes to sitting tenants, more commonly to new, more affluent clients. Throughout the 1960s, a large number of initially small property companies came into being, seeking out and buying up much of the rented accommodation held by trusts or managed by local agents for absentee landlords. As one of the so-called 'break-up' specialists put it:

> the economics of break-up are that the dealer buys blocks on the basis of about two-thirds of market value on empty units; one-third market value on tenanted units. The dealer can thus sell the empty units on the open market as soon as buyers can be found; his profit on those units is 50%, less expenses and the temporary financing costs.[19]

Thus, the old stock of rented property was progressively acquired sometimes for site values, sometimes for renovation and reletting and sometimes for sale to owner-occupiers. In the process, the stratum of individual landlords gave way more and more to property entrepreneurs, some of whose companies expanded and penetrated local housing markets from one end of the country to another. In our own study, and in that made by the Benwell CDP team,[20] the emergence of new property company landlords and the spread of their operations was very plain.

The attempts by successive governments in the 1960s to eradicate slum housing, the encouragement given to local authorities for programmes of 'comprehensive redevelopment' or 'urban renewal', all too often served simply to stimulate speculative activity on the part both of the very large development companies and also of the smaller entrepreneurs with interests in domestic property. Recognizing the vulnerability of young families and individuals moving into the cities, or the especial weaknesses of the New Commonwealth immigrants, some of the latter sought to remove the old tenants who generally were paying very small rents, and replace them with those whose housing needs were desperate or those with the capital and incomes to buy at inflated prices. A term was coined to describe the craft of forcing people out of their tenancies: 'winkling' it was called. Often it was a very unsubtle process as the Royal Commission of London's Housing revealed.[21] Later in the decade when grants for the rehabilitation of older property were introduced, many middle-class couples were encouraged to look for large houses in run-down, former middle-class suburbs relatively close to the city centres. In some areas this process of 'gentrification' produced sharp confrontations between the established locals on one side, and the property companies and the incomers on the other. In a report prepared by a neighbourhood law centre, the pressures exerted on tenants to get them to leave were described in considerable detail. In one case a family had resisted the threats and blandishments of their landlord for two years but when their house was acquired by another property company, they found that the bulging front wall had become the excuse for some altogether tougher tactics:

> On a Monday in July, while both Mr and Mrs Murphy were out, builders entered the house and demolished the outer wall of their living room and bedroom leaving them exposed to the elements and to the full view of the street – rather like an open-fronted doll's house. A builder's 'Acro', a steel support, was erected from the middle of the *bed* to the ceiling under the roof to stop it caving in.[22]

Such was the determination of the Murphys and others in this street in Barnsbury that the property dealers were eventually driven to sell their properties to the council; but not before they had already made some nice profits on those properties they had emptied and resold.

The first of the post-war booms in Britain saw some enormous fortunes made from property development and speculation. A few of the entrepreneurs, like Jack Cotton, had begun their property careers in the 1930s but most were newcomers to the business. Marriott's data suggest that the great majority of these 'buccaneers' learned about the real estate markets in the offices of estate agents or else were building contractors or solicitors experienced in property conveyancing. Initially, the companies they founded or bought over were run in a highly personal way, the crucial decisions about land purchase or the nature of the development being taken by the aspiring 'impresarios' themselves. Men like Walter Flack of Murrayfield Real Estate or Harry Hyams of Oldham Estates negotiated with the local councils or with financial backers face to face. Their involvement in the transactions was immediate, their control of their enterprises direct. But gradually this 'entrepreneurial' phase gave way by the end of the 1960s to another more complex 'corporate' stage of development. In order to carry out their increasingly grandiose schemes for office construction or hotel building or central-city redevelopment, the property tycoons began to consolidate the assets of several companies. There were mergers and take-overs in which small concerns became absorbed into larger and larger agglomerations of property capital. Some of the developers, in order to raise sufficient finance, entered into alliances with large builders, as Hyams did with Wimpey Construction. Joint companies were established linking Cotton's City Centre Properties to Woolworths or Shell with the intention of gaining access to sites or meeting potential needs for trading or office accommodation.[23] There were increasingly formalized links with banks, insurance companies and other institutions with money to invest. Though the process is not well documented in Britain, the growth in the size of the property companies produced changes in the patterns of management not unlike those described by Lorimer. The entrepreneurs remained important but the day-to-day work of running the companies with their large portfolios of property holdings, their diverse sources of rental income, their now widely spread, often international dealings, passed more and more into the hands of professional managers. As a director of one of the companies with large-scale aspirations observed:

> Property development can no longer be regarded as the last refuge of the entrepreneur. While conceptual and entrepreneurial ability is still important and financial acumen is indispensable, technical, sociological and political considerations are of equal importance.[24]

Following the consolidation of property holdings, the collapse of the property market in 1974, the taxes and restrictions on development imposed by government and the general slow-down of economic activity in the late 1970s, the property companies contrived to manage their affairs in altogether less spectacular ways. Today the property business is dominated by immensely wealthy corporations which, while not eschewing opportunites for speculation, appear mainly interested in steady long-term profitability. Their often flamboyant, much publicized founders, the Cottons, Clores, Hyams, Sterns and others have passed away or slid from view. The largely anonymous managers have taken over.

Finance

At the point at which many of the development companies and the domestic property companies were founded, the sums of money required to launch a property career were often modest. Especially for those involved in domestic housing market a few hundred pounds was all that many of the jobbing builders or the aspiring landlords needed and throughout the 1950s and 1960s many of the new property companies, which we traced in our own study, appear to have raised the finances from their own pockets or from those of family and friends.[25] Even the purchase of existing property companies could be arranged for comparatively small amounts – Hyams paid only £22,000 for the Oldham Estate Company in 1958. At that stage, there was still much neglected, undervalued property, especially in the form of old rented housing or run-down industrial buildings. But as the ambitions of the property owners and dealers grew, so the need for other sources of funds became more acute. Those who wished to develop sites for offices or shops and those who could plan to refurbish and relet domestic property soon found that the banks shared their appraisal of the prospects for profit and advanced money at what were, in the early 1960s, low rates of interest and in generous amounts. As Jack Rose, author of the 'Valuers' Bible' and long an associate of some of the most successful property entrepreneurs explained recently, the first boom owed much to

> the simple financial formula whereby a mortgage of two-thirds of the value of the completed building would cover the total costs of the site plus the building itself, fees and interest during the development period. This meant the developer did not need to keep any of his own money in the project. More important, he would be left with a surplus of income after deducting the mortgage interest from the rent. This condition . . . allowed individuals to undertake one development after another.[26]

However, when the property bubble burst in 1974, companies carrying very large mortgages, faced with rising interest rates and inflation, and unable to sell their assets, found themselves in considerable difficulties. Many went bankrupt. Suddenly there was a new atmosphere of caution. The banks, especially the big five, became much more wary about advancing money to property dealers and these entrepreneurs themselves were not eager to assume large burdens of debt a second time.

But while the development companies greatly reduced the scale of their activities and were forced, as often they were, to sell off large parts of their assets in attempts to weather the economic storm, others in the property business increased their involvement. For the prospects of profit were still there. From 1974 to 1977 rents for offices or commercial property went on rising (except in London) and even in 1974 and 1975 the values of property shares stayed well ahead of general share values. For the developers, retrenchment was the order of the day but for institutional investors, the insurance companies and the pension funds and for the development subsidiaries of the construction firms and the nationalized industries like British Rail, there were enhanced opportunities. With enormous sums to invest, the insurance companies and the pension funds stood to benefit from the availability of property – the completed projects and the sites put on the market by the overstretched developers. Compared with the returns on investment in manufacturing industry in Britain, property ownership and property development offered good returns. Thus, throughout the 1970s, we can see a rapid growth in the levels of property investment on the part of the institutions. Insurance companies put £198 million into commercial property in 1970 and £406 million in 1975. Pension fund investment in forms of real estate rose from £97 million in 1970 to £342 million in 1975 and by 1978 their enthusiasm for property was such that the level of their investment had surpassed that of the insurance companies: they invested £591 million, the insurance companies £549 million.

Some important changes in the structure of the property market have been taking place. More and more projects are undertaken by financial institutions and development companies acting in partnership. And the initiative, the investment 'push' and the direction of development are increasingly provided by the managers of the pension funds or the insurance companies' property specialists. In 1979, for example, the Norwich Union Insurance Company joined forces with Town and City and Freehold and Leasehold Properties to create a £20 million complex of shops and offices in London's Cambridge Circus. Elsewhere, insurance companies, pension funds and the property development experts of public enterprises have formed consortia for office building as in the recent Norwich Union, ICI pension funds and British Rail complex at Euston Station. The pension funds are currently the most aggressive force in the property market. The Electricity Supply Nominees who manage the pension funds of employees of the Electricity Council, have well over £100 million invested in property and in partnership with the developers, Stock Conversion, are undertaking the redevelopment of the famous Trocadero site in Piccadilly, are planning to take sole responsibility for the construction of a massive new shopping centre in Wood Green in North London, and have lately extended their operations to retail development in California and Arizona. In the past twenty years, the National Coal Board's pension funds have grown from less than £5 million to £200 million, and their annual income in 1976 was £15 million, 30 per cent of it from property. The fund owns offices, shopping centres, industrial property, luxury flats, television centres, pubs, clubs, petrol stations and multi-storey car parks. In 1977, the Gas Board pension fund paid £17 million for seventy-six empty shops. The Post Office Superannuation Fund has existed since 1970, and already by 1975 had a property investment portfolio of £85 million, and owned 15.5 per cent of Argyle Securities.

Thus, the property market in Britain is increasingly dominated by large financial institutions and in a period of recession and high interest rates, it is likely that this will become even more marked. Many companies seeking to refurbish their premises or move to new ones find it advantageous to unlock some of their assets by selling off their existing sites and buildings. 'Sale and leaseback' schemes have become noticeably popular in prime high-street locations and on many of the industrial estates. Those to whom they sell are often the financial institutions and their developer allies. And as the opportunity to acquire the most profitable forms of property – the office blocks, the shopping complexes, the factories and warehouses – shrinks, as it does when so much of it is salted away in their long-term portfolios, so the institutional investors will move into the so-called 'secondary' markets. Commercial properties, offices and some forms of domestic housing which, with some modernisation, offer the prospects of higher levels of rent, will be added (as is already happening) to the holdings of these companies and funds. And these concentrations of capital should not be seen as sharply differentiated from the traditional providers of finance, for though pension funds do mobilize the contributions of thousands of employees, this does not mean that we are confronting some radical new forms of ownership. Though he does not deal in any detail with their real estate activities, Richard Minns's[27] analysis of British pension funds shows that there are few instances where the workers in private or public enterprises have any real influence on the investment decisions which direct the flows of their funds. Both the insurance companies and the pension funds have been successfully incorporated by the established institutions of finance capital: the merchant and joint stock banks, the unit trust managers and the stockbrokers. Thus, recent changes in the property market have been such as to increase the power and influence of the financial establishments in an area of operation that, like many other sectors of our economies, was once much more highly differentiated and localized.

Owner-occupation

From the foregoing account, it is easy to see that urban land and real estate can constitute an important source of profit and power for development entrepreneurs and for financial institutions. But alongside all the grandiose schemes for offices and shopping complexes, other changes have been taking place which have even more immediate and obvious impact on the day-to-day lives of citizens. In Britain since the war, the political commitment to a 'property-owning democracy' has been expressed chiefly through government encouragement of owner-occupation, and as we observed earlier, the speed at which owner-occupation has grown is quite remarkable. Today more than 53 per cent of all households live in a home they own or are in the process of purchasing.[28] A question which has repeatedly been asked is: does this simple change have any wider social, political or economic implications? There are two broad schools of thought on the matter. In the 1950s and 1960s some writers linked owner-occupation with other changes – like the movement of populations to the suburbs – and argued that becoming a property owner along with other alterations to the family's or individual's economic circumstances did produce differences of attitude and values. The new owner-occupiers, they argued became more conservative in their opinions, more home and family centred, less conscious – if they were manual workers – of working-class membership.[29] There was much *naïveté* and exaggeration in these accounts and many criticized such views on the grounds that there was neither empirical evidence nor adequate theory to support crude notions of 'embourgeoisement'. However, the conviction persisted that different tenure groups had noticeably different economic interests and opportunities and that these interests helped to structure the actual patterns of day-to-day interaction. And that was hardly unreasonable, for examples of competition and conflict between owner-occupiers and tenants, especially tenants in public housing, abounded.[30] Through the 1960s and the 1970s studies of residential segregation and of hostility and local political action organized around public versus private housing accumulated.[31] In their study of race and housing in Birmingham, Rex and Moore took the ill-formulated notions of diverse housing interests and tried to construct an anlysis of conflict in the city which revolved around the idea that there were discrete 'housing classes' – groups differentially located in the markets and allocative systems for housing.[32]

The fact that Weber saw class as dependent upon market situation and that he distinguished more than one form of property led Rex and Moore to argue that within the city, groups and individuals could be distinguished not only in terms of their position and interests in the processes of production, but also in terms of their location in the market for housing. There are several slightly different versions of the 'housing-class' model offered by the authors but essentially the claim is that there are several different 'classes' ranging from the outright owners of desirable homes in the suburbs through those buying flats and houses on mortgages, the tenants of purpose-built council housing to lodging-house owners and at the bottom, tenants of single rooms in those subdivided lodgings.[33]

The scheme has received a good deal of criticism over the years, the most important of which is the argument that a strictly Weberian view should lead to a focus on domestic property as a means of generating income. That is, we should ask: In what ways does domestic property ownership confer economic opportunities? How does it determine life chances? What does it offer in terms of real gains? Obviously for landlords, for property dealers and developers, domestic property does have the character of a real, productive resource. They are part of an advantaged class of property owners and it would seem that those who merely rent or buy from them, who are dependent upon them, constitute a subordinate 'property class'. But Rex and Moore's analysis does not deal with property relations in this way. There is very little said about such obvious clashes of economic interest since the analysis generally focuses on what are essentially status differences between tenure groups, documenting the patterns of competition and alliance and political mobilisation that occur. Haddon[34] argues that the 'housing-class' scheme is inadequate because it fails to see that there is a difference between housing as an item of consumption – as something that is an integral part of a life style, as something that helps define a status group – and housing as a marketable commodity from which revenues and profits can be obtained. There is no doubt that as it stands, the Rex and Moore model simply will not do.

However, the basic insight that domestic property might, like other forms of property, be looked at in terms of its potential for economic returns should not be dismissed lightly, for as Saunders has recently pointed out, housing does have two faces. It is at one and the same time both an item of individual consumption and a means whereby economic gains may be made. The implications of this are considerable. As Saunders puts it:

> if house ownership can be shown to provide access to a source of real accumulation, then from a Weberian perspective, owner-occupation must be recognised as a basis for the formation of property classes, and political action on the part of home owners . . . cannot be explained in terms of mere status identification.[35]

Demonstrating that owner-occupation, at least over the last twenty-five or thirty years, has produced 'real accumulation' is exactly what he tries to do. Combatting a series of well-known objections to the idea that the gains made by individual home owners have any wide significance, Saunders shows that housing can be the source of considerable economic privilege. His argument rests essentially on three claims. First, he points to the fact that since the war there has been very considerable inflation in house prices and that money invested in a house has given better returns than almost any other form of investment. It is not adequate to argue that this is simply forced savings and that a non-owner could make comparable gains through other forms of investment thus obviating any significant difference between the two. The fact is that the rate of inflation of house prices has, over thirty years, far exceeded that of other investments. Thus, differential inflation rates have generated bonuses for house owners. It is true, of course, that the house owner who sells his property and realizes a substantial gain is doing so partly at the expense of the first-time buyer. But that is simply to say that part of the accumulation comes in the form of a premium paid by the hitherto excluded 'non-owner' for membership of the advantaged class.

Even more recently, Mary Farmer illustrated the point by calculating that

An own-house speculator . . . who bought an average house in 1965, could have turned an initial deposit of £1,000 into £28,000 by moving every three years and borrowing the average amount building societies were allowing new buyers in the relevant years. This is a real return of 15.7 per cent.[36]

A second factor to be considered is the very favourable rate of interest on which mortgages have been given. Home ownership is such a politically sensitive issue that successive governments have persuaded building societies to keep their rates low and have even provided direct subsidies to achieve that end. Even without government cajoling, the societies have held their rates far below the general level of inflation. In effect, says Saunders, owner-occupiers have borrowed money at substantial negative rates of interest and this has been achieved at the expense of building society investors, most of whom are less wealthy than the borrowers.

Third, there is the subsidy for house ownership provided by tax allowances given on mortgages. In some years, as the figures provided by the Department of the Environment show,[37] the subsidies for house owners exceed those given to council tenants. Taken together, these three factors ensure that housing provides a means of acquiring wealth considerably in excess of that which would be available to a private or council tenant.

It is sometimes objected that this kind of wealth accumulation is illusory since it cannot readily be converted into cash. All too often the 'gain' is made only after the death of the house owner when the property can be sold. But that argument is weak if judged against the empirical evidence. The fact is, many owners when selling one house on which they have made a considerable capital gain, hold back part of that surplus when buying their next house. In this way, they realize the cash value of some of their accumulation immediately. Even if they choose to reinvest all the 'gain' in their next house, they will be enabled to acquire a new and generally larger mortgage on a more valuable asset and, of course, the higher the mortgage the greater the tax relief it attracts. Apart from these considerations, there is the unchallengeable fact that the ownership of property, even if it is on a mortgage, confers eligibility for credit. It is a hall-mark of financial stability.

Thus, it becomes increasingly clear that domestic property is both an item of consumption and a very important means of accumulation.

During periods of financial stringency when governments attempt to hold down wage and salary levels by statutory means or social compacts, the relative significance of property ownership has increased greatly. For the owners of housing the importance of what is generally their largest asset has been made more salient as its value grows, while income from employment has been held static or has even fallen back in real terms in some recent years. To argue, as some Marxists do, that there are really no conflicts of interest between owner-occupiers and tenants is hardly credible if we accept this analysis.

The role of the state

The changing physical and social structure of our cities, then, has to be accounted for in large measure by the operation of market forces. The building of office complexes, of retail facilities, of warehouses and factories, the sprawl of suburban private housing or the 'gentrification' of inner-city areas – all these have been stimulated by the quest for corporate or individual profit. But this takes place in a context. Britain's is a mixed economy, one in which the state nationally and locally plays a major part in stimulating or inhibiting economic activity, expanding or restricting the opportunities for production and consumption.

In terms of urban development, we can see the state acting in ways which have considerably altered the housing stock, the availability of land, the rights of property owners – in short, the whole complex of the built environment. The state has acted positively to encourage first, the building of large stocks of public housing (which was a major commitment of the Labour Government immediately after the war) and somewhat later, the provision of owner-occupied housing. Contracts for the construction of council housing, ranging from the vast suburban estates and the high-rise apartments of the 1950s and 1960s to the more selective programmes of infilling and rehabilitation in the 1970s, have provided work for architects, lawyers, estate agents and builders up and down the country. Until the economic squeezes of the mid-1970s, such work provided an important underpinning of the economic activities of those in the property business in Britain.

Centrally and locally, governments in the first two decades after 1945 did much to stimulate office construction and even after restrictions were imposed on such projects in London, the developers and builders received encouragement and assistance to continue this work in the provincial centres. The granting or withholding of planning permission, political decisions about densities or designs, these affected the prospects of the property entrepreneurs in obvious ways. The actions of the city planners and engineers and their political masters contributed, as we have seen, to the profitability of particular development or building firms, but more than that, they tended, in their aggregate effect, to facilitate the growth of a large and increasingly concentrated development industry. The agencies of governments even became major customers for the office builders, contributing from the public purse large sums for the rent of office space. In Britain as elsewhere in the west, the state and the city and regional governments have acted in many ways to support the expansion of the development industry, seeing this as necessary for economic growth and the attainment of political and social goals.

But these public authorities have not shown the same face to all forms of property owner. Labour governments in particular have acted to restrict the rights of private landlords, to defend the tenants against excessive rent increases and to extend the occupier's rights of tenure. Tory administrations have generally acted to ease controls over private landlords, arguing that unless there are better prospects for reasonable returns or 'fair' rents, the stock of privately rented accommodation will simply dry up. But for all the rhetoric, Conservative governments have not seriously undermined the legislative restrictions on private rented property. The very dramatic decline in private landlordsim has weakened the associations of landlords seeking representation of their interest in the Tory party and widely publicized cases of landlords harassing their tenants, or asking for excessively high payments, undermines the will even of Tory governments to champion the landlords' cause. On the left, the shrinkage of the private rental sector can be used to buttress the argument that this is an unacceptable, indeed an anachronistic form of tenure and one that will shortly all but disappear.

With the election of the Thatcher government, the role of the state in urban development may well change more sharply than in previous years. The ideological commitment to 'rolling back the state' and to the stimulation of free enterprise is already producing some important effects. First, there is a retreat from public responsibility for housing large sections of the working class. The cuts in local authority grants have brought council house building to a virtual standstill and greatly reduced the funds for maintenance and rehabilitation. It is the declared intention of central government to force all local authorities to offer council houses for sale with the anticipated long-term effect that the stock of public housing will be significantly reduced.

There is also a publicly declared intention to reduce 'red tape' and lift many forms of planning control over house building and smaller commercial projects on the supposition that planning restrictions have hampered economic growth (an unproven assumption, this) and the expectation that free market forces will lead to economic regeneration. Such a philosophy underlies the creation of 'enterprise zones' within which firms will not only be allowed to offset 100 per cent of their capital expenditure against tax but they will also be free from the Development Land Tax and from many planning controls.

And beyond that, there is the so-called 'sale of the century' in which public assets, including much urban real estate will be sold to private enterprise.[38] This will certainly affect the new towns which will be forced to sell off their revenue-producing properties – the shopping centres and the leased industrial sites – thereby losing their chief means of servicing their massive capital loans. Along with the winding up of the New Town Commission which hitherto acquired such assets when individual New Town Corporations reached maturity, such a scheme will serve greatly to weaken the New Town movement. On the other hand, it will help to fuel what property developers already see as an imminent property boom. Already they and the pension fund and insurance company managers are preparing their bids for these lucrative public assets.

Thus, market forces and political practices are intimately interwoven in the modern economy. Over the past thirty years, the character of the property market and of property relations have changed and these changes have a most important bearing on the nature of community politics and patterns of local protest. And that is the subject of our next chapter.

Chapter 6

Power and Protest in the City

The cities of the west have been noisy places in recent years. Throughout the 1960s and the 1970s they provided the arenas for a great many collective agitations: from the racial violence of American cities or the celebrated riots of May 1968 in Paris, to the most diverse array of demonstrations and protests by squatters, council house tenants, ratepayers, environmentalists and others. The action has been channelled through national political parties, local political groups, residents' associations, community action committees and a host of *ad hoc* organisations.

It is important not to exaggerate the extent of the novelty of popular urban unrest. Cities have always offered important stages for the expression of indignation and discontent, for the simple reason that they provide the elementary preconditions for collective action. They bring people together, encourage processes of differentiation, concentrate and make visible shared interests and as local 'polities' and the centres of local 'economies', contain the principal targets of the protestors, the local politicians, local public officials and local representatives of capital. However, it does seem that in the last two decades, the volume of contestatory action in the cities has been especially high, so high that in the view of Castells, urban struggles are now at the heart of political conflict in many capitalist societies.[1] How then should we account for all this noise? It seems likely that it signals some profound dissatisfactions and probably some important shifts in the patterns of social relations. In this chapter, we shall focus on three things: on some major changes in social structure; on the weaknesses of prevailing systems of representation; on the emergence of new issues in urban politics.

Changes in social structure

We can sketch the most important changes by looking briefly at the occupational structure. The 'post-industrial society' writers like Bell and Touraine[2] have drawn attention to a number of the most obvious shifts that have occurred in the structures of western societies in the post-war period.

First, there is the decline of the manufacturing sector, in relative terms, which has meant that today there are proportionally fewer workers engaged in 'blue-collar' jobs. The general movement towards what is frequently described as a 'service' economy has the effect of eroding the traditional base of proletarian life. Today, many of the unskilled or semi-skilled jobs in the economy are found not in factories, mills and mines, but in service industries or public service organisations. At the same time, employment in primary industries and in agriculture continues the processes of contraction that have been in train for many years.

By contrast, there has been an enormous expansion of routine white-collar work in the economy. The demand for all kinds of clerical and minor supervisory skills grew rapidly in the post-war years as the bureaucratisation of industry and of much public sector activity accelerated. As the numbers grew and as technological changes in office work routinized many clerical and white-collar tasks, so the job situations of these workers became more obviously like those of the traditional blue-collar workers. By the mid-1960s, demand for clerical employees levelled out, minimally skilled white-collar work was effectively 'proletarianised' and as if in partial recognition of this, white-collar unionism began the rapid increase which it sustained through the 1970s and 'industrial' action modelled on the tactics of the old industrial unions became more and more common.[3] Over the past thirty years, many manual workers have found themselves latterly doing non-manual jobs and even more commonly, many have seen their sons and daughters employed in this way. Intra- or inter-generationally they have crossed a very important line in the social structure, for though they cannot be held to be 'upwardly mobile' in any very major way (the increasing similarity of work situations should be taken seriously), such a translation does lead to involvement in social *mileux* which in the past have had different material conditions – better security and more perks, if not more pay – and different histories of collective action.[4] The overall effect of these changes is to increase the internal differentiation of the working class; they add to the existing, long-standing divisions based on skills, patterns of union organisation and levels of reward.

In the British working class today, there are considerable differences in levels of material well-being and little evidence that overall changes in earning capacities have led to any significant upgrading of the relative position of the poorest groups in recent years.[5] Status differences in the British working class remain important, manifesting themselves in disputes about 'differentials' or in complaints about the movement of less 'respectable' families into 'desirable' public housing areas.[6]

Most importantly, though, the working class is, today, divided by race. In the last twenty years there has been created in Britain an underclass, a pool of imported cheap labour without which transport, the health services and parts of the textile industry would be difficult to operate. Increasingly, the black population is being forced to defend its interests through separate associations and movements. The failure of the unions and the labour movement to defend the black workers is leading, as Rex has recently pointed out,[7] to more comprehensive and more militant defensive organisations. The sense of rejection that blacks have come to feel as a result of their dealings with white trades unions, the suspicion with which the Labour Party and leftist groups are viewed is very evident from the most cursory reading of the black press.[8]

The middle class has also changed in recent years.[9] It has, by most conventional measures, become both larger and more diverse, for although parts of the traditional petit-bourgeoisie have declined, these losses have been more than offset by substantial growth in the professional and technically trained workforce and the expansion of managerial positions. There can be little doubt that it is the rapid rise in the numbers of professionals – the doctors, scientists and other 'health care' workers, the teachers and researchers at universities and colleges, the school teachers, the scientific and technical workers in industry and civil service, the planners, co-ordinators and administrators in private and public enterprises – that constitutes the most important change.

Today, in all western economies there is a new group, a stratum with no satisfactory name, distinguished by its possession of technical skills and expertise. It consists of those whose 'capacity for income' rests on their knowledge, on their specialized education. It is a stratum whose growth was encouraged by the political decisions of the 1950s and 1960s: the decisions greatly to expand the educational systems, to encourage economic growth through the development and application of technical knowledge, and to extend in very major ways the role of the state in the management of the economy and in the provision of services to the citizens. Viewed historically, it appears as a rising stratum, one which seeks in diverse ways to extend its power and to ensure the conditions of its reproduction and expansion. Most frequently, it is aligned with the dominant capitalist interests of our economy, finding the conditions of its advancement in its capacity to 'service' the needs of industry or the demands of those controlling the agencies of the state, but it is not confined to a supportive role. In its own ranks, there is a bureaucratised intelligentsia, some fragments of which generate critiques of existing social and economic and political arrangements, identify the divergences of interests of this and other strata and from time to time, encourage action to procure the advancement of the rising 'service' stratum.   These broad changes in the *national* arrangements of the social structure are reflected in the social composition and in the struggles for power observed at *local* levels. The social characteristics of cities and regions, of districts and neighbourhoods have changed, partly in response to the secular trends and partly as a consequence of deliberate contrivance by those in positions of economic and political influence. Business organisations, especially those concerned with economic and real estate development, from time to time produce very explicit statements of their concern to engineer, at local levels, a change in the social mix. Take, for example, the following observation of an association much embroiled in an important urban development programme in San Francisco:

If San Francisco decides to compete effectively with other cities for new 'clean' industries and new corporate power, its population will move closer to standard White-Anglo-Saxon-Protestant characteristics. As automation increases, the need for unskilled labour will decrease. Economically and socially the population will tend to range from lower middle class through lower upper class . . . Selection of a population's composition might be undemocratic. Influence on it, however, is legal and desirable for the health of the city. A workable, though changing balance of economic levels, social types, age levels and other factors must be maintained. Influence on these factors should be exerted in many ways, for example, changing the quality of housing, schools and job opportunities.[10]

Such arguments were deployed in order to further the ambitions of property developers and their business allies, to oust a relatively poor population from the inner city and to have its homes and places of recreation and employment replaced by the office blocks, hotels, conference centres and other institutions offering job opportunities for the 'new' middle class and profits for the property entrepreneurs. The immediate issue was a shift in the nature of one particular neighbourhood but the statement makes clear that this was conceived as contributing to the alteration of the social structure of a much wider area.

Elsewhere in North America we can find evidence of the ways in which secular changes in occupational and economic patterns produce changes in the political life of cities. In David Ley's study of Vancouver we can see just how a new elite, recruited from the ranks of the 'service' class, opposed and for a while replaced the traditional local rulership of business owners and property development 'boosters'.[11] Over the 1950s and 1960s and 1970s, the social composition of Vancouver altered dramatically. The city grew very rapidly and while many new blue-collar jobs were created the most startling expansion took place in white-collar work. By 1971, 70 per cent of the occupations in the city were white-collar ones and from 1951 to 1971, Ley argues, the number of professional and technical jobs doubled. From 1971 to 1975 the number of jobs in the city advanced roughly 8,000 a year, some 75 per cent of these being the result of new office construction. Vancouver became the 'service' or 'post-industrial' city *par excellence*. In 1968 a new political body was formed, a new 'party' (The Electors' Action Movement) set up to challenge the established power of the right-wing Non-Partisan Association which was dominated by business and most especially property development interests. The new party articulated what Ley calls a 'liberal ideology', portraying itself as the vehicle of a reform movement seeking to contest the 'growth above all' philosophy and the 'city efficient' ideas of the old guard. TEAM supporters were recruited very heavily from the ranks of the professionals, over a third of those surveyed in one study were indentified as such, and among their ranks lawyers, university professors, teachers and architects were especially prominent. TEAM promised to create 'the liveable city', to put human and aesthetic considerations above mere profit and growth. TEAM mobilized and expressed the concerns of a highly educated elite recruited from the ranks of the professionals and the technically qualified (four of the eight TEAM aldermen in 1972 were university professors) but it did so in the name of the citizenry at large.

It provided a nice case of a rising stratum seeking to complement the social honour and the economic power which it enjoyed, by the acquisition of political leverage. It was engaged in a process of wresting control of the council and its agencies from the speculators and developers and other business proprietors in order to supplant their material interests with their own particular mix of social and intellectual concerns. As with most changes of this kind, political success depended on selling the ideas of this group to a wider population. Once in power though, as Ley records, the politics of the new party proved to be 'elitist' and confronted unforeseen problems of social justice. The benefits of the 'city liveable' soon showed themselves to be subject to the manipulations of the market. Those who gained most from the improvements in environmental quality were not the poorer 'east siders'. By the late 1970s, TEAM was in disarray and in 1978 it lost heavily in the municipal elections:

> TEAM's commitment to pluralism, open government, and the liveable city overlooked, or perhaps presupposed, the achievement both of equity and also economic security. In the union which it forged between cultural and political realms there was the conceptual and also political failure to treat economic relations as problematic . . . As a result TEAM policies were able to promote the conditions for a liveable city more easily than they could equitably allocate the ensuing benefits.[12]

In Britain, where local politics are much more closely bound to the national party structure, where the major battles are between Tories and Labour, the effects of changes in local social structures are less easily seen. The formation of new parties to contest local elections, though by no means unknown, has been less important than the process (a much more opaque one, it has to be said) of change in the recruitment of personnel *within* the existing party organisations. Although to our knowledge, there exists no major nation-wide study of the changing patterns of local party recruitment there are indications that here too, as we argued in an earlier chapter, the role of those from the so-called 'service class' is of growing importance and helps to make sense of conflicts inside the parties (especially the Labour Party) and the emergence of new policies.[13]

The important point is this: that to understand the nature of contemporary urban politics and to 'explain' recent or current agitations, we need to keep a sharp eye on changes in the class and status structures of the whole society and on the local manifestations of these changes.

Problems of representation

In the past thirty years there have been important changes in the composition of activists and elected representatives of political parties in Britain. The changes are observable at both local and at national levels.[14] In local politics the non-partisan associations and the 'independent' councillors have generally been replaced by representatives of national parties and inside the local Tory, Liberal or Labour groups, struggles for power have been going on between 'old guards' and 'young turks'. In the right-wing associations and often in the local Tory parties it is possible to see members of the 'new' middle class – the professionals and the technically qualified – replacing the groupings of local entrepreneurs. In the local Labour parties very similar developments have been afoot. Traditional political elites recruited from the trades unions and from among long-serving, working-class Labour party members have in many districts and many councils, been replaced or at least challenged by men and women who typically are younger, more highly educated and in professional or semi-professional jobs and who frequently portray themselves as markedly more 'radical' than the old stagers. The rise of the Social Democratic Party and its involvement in local as well as national politics may cast further light on the political interests and aspirations of the 'rising stratum', for though it is far too early to pronounce on the matter with any confidence, it does appear that the new party is drawing substantial support from this quarter. If the new party sustains its momentum we may well see emerging from it and its allies a 'liberal ideology' and a social democratic presence which will have some impact on the town halls.

In both the major parties, and at all levels, we can trace the incursions of those who come from the 'service' class and in some instances the scale of their advance is such as to establish their domination of the local party. Where this is true, serious tensions arise, for the 'old guards' claim that under the new regime their interests and those of whole strata are no longer adequately represented. Thus, a good many petit-bourgeois look with dismay on the neglect of their interests by the 'technocratic' middle-class elements in local Tory parties and nurse much resentment over their loss of power in the party or the council. And at the other end of the political spectrum, established working-class councillors or party activists are no better pleased, feeling themselves shouldered aside by the products of the colleges and universities with their Labour clubs or Marxist groupings. As Hindess, Forester and others have observed, there has been an important shift in the character of local Labour parties; a shift which generally has left the working-class members with a sense that 'their' party has been taken over. Today, the teachers, academics and social workers appear, in many constituencies and local groups, to have manoeuvred themselves into positions of influence and control. Often they represent themselves as a 'reforming' element, intent upon the destruction of the traditional forms of patronage and the petty corruption found among some of the established cliques[15] and determined to replace pragmatic and accommodative policies with more heavily theorized, ideological politics. Both major parties are broad coalitions but in recent years both have experienced changes of personnel and policy which produce a sense of 'disenfranchisement' among some of their traditional supporters.

There is also another sector of the population which has reason to be cynical about the existing systems of representation: the immigrants, especially the non-white immigrants. Governments at all levels and of all complexions, in Britain, pay lip-service to the idea of racial equality but in practice they are more responsive to the fears of the white majority than to the needs of the ethnic minorities. The 3.2 million New Commonwealth immigrants are poorly represented inside the major political parties and at local levels they have experienced in multifarious ways the prejudice and hostility that lurks in working-class no less than middle-class districts. The Labour Party and the trades unions might seem the natural champions of the many thousands of black workers in cities like London, Leicester, Birmingham and Bradford but in government, Labour has passed immigration laws whose illiberal character could not be concealed by the accompanying race relations legislation and the unions all too often have failed to support the struggles of blacks in industry.[16] In consequence, there is in the black communities much mistrust of the major institutions which serve to represent the interests of the poor or the proletarian.

People voice their discontents in whatever way they can. If they feel themselves excluded from or forced to play only a very subordinate role in the main political institutions, they will contrive to have their grievances heard some other way. They will move outside the parties and the unions and seek new avenues for participation or maybe, for protest. And that surely is what has been happening over the past decade or so in our cities, as the working-class inhabitants of dreary and neglected public housing schemes formed their community associations, as groups of mobile youngsters and others who were homeless, established their squatting organisations and other bodies to lobby or defend them. Most of the associations have been formed locally. It has been local sentiments that, in the first instance, have been mobilized, but magazines like *Community Action* and organisations like Shelter indicate the national significance of these parochial expressions of discontent.

Owner-occupiers in many localities form themselves into 'parties' – residents' associations or ratepayers' associations – to defend themselves against increased taxation, to protect their property values or to maintain the social boundaries of their neighbourhoods. Ratepayers' groups, proclaiming their non-partisanship enter the political arena directly and in recent years there have been attempts to deliver their support to more militant class-based organisations. At the height of the 1973–4 inflationary crisis, there were threats of 'rate strikes' and one of the national leaders of the ratepayers' groups approached General Walker and his Civil Assistance organisation with the aim of making ratepayers' associations part of the envisaged network of 'apprehensive patriots' available to ensure that essential services were maintained in the event of a general strike. Up and down the country in the period between 1974 and 1979, new associations of bourgeois elements appeared urging the 're-education' of the middle class and action to defend the material and moral interests of what they like to depict as neglected, voiceless constituencies of the 'middle class'.[17]

Among the black population too, the representation of interests has been occurring outside the conventional framework of party politics. In order to negotiate the rules of, say, the local public housing bureaucracies, or to pressure the education authorities, groups of black citizens have set up their own ethnically based associations, like the Bengali Housing Association or the Bradford Black Collective. In the workplace too, separate bodies to express the hopes and fears of non-whites have appeared (the Asian Workers' Association, for example) and as the tide of racial abuse and attack has risen,[18] incited by the National Front or the British Movement, so community-based defence associations have appeared.[19]

The growth of the new modes of representation, the appearance of defiant or contestatory action among the citizenry owes a good deal, in our opinion, to the expansion of the so-called 'service' class and particularly to the bureaucratised intelligentsia whose ranks have swollen with the rapid development of educational and cultural services. Some segments of this intelligentsia have been engaged in a process which Jeane Kirkpatrick[20] refers to as the 'demoralising' of contemporary capitalist society. By this she means that they have been making explicit and holding up for criticism, the beliefs and loyalties that hold such a society together. In literature and drama, no less than in social and political writings, the exploitative nature of much capitalist activity at home and abroad has been laid bare. The intelligentsia have made possible the 'penetration' of social and economic structures and stirred awareness of their subordination among many ordinary people. Bell argues that there has grown up an 'adversary culture' among the large stratum of highly educated men and women produced by our universities and colleges over the past twenty years.[21] This is not to claim that they are offering any specifically leftist alternative: few among them do that. But the dissemination of their misgivings about capitalism nourishes an extensive disenchantment and licenses many forms of defiant behaviour. With their help, the values and institutions which sustain deference and docility have been challenged and broken both by structural and ideological developments in the past few years. Thus, we can observe that many 'who find themselves in subordinate positions, and notably those who work in factories, mines, offices, shops, schools, hospitals and so on, do what they can to mitigate, resist and transform the conditions of their subordination'.[22] They are encouraged in this by members of the new 'service' stratum. The state of 'de-subordination' of which Miliband writes owes a good deal to the efforts of the intelligentsia within this new stratum. Inspiration or assistance, leadership and organisation of many forms of popular protest are undertaken by its members.

The growth of so many new 'political' associations, the maintenance of lobbies, the periodic demonstrations and public meetings can be seen as responses to the failure of the established parties: their failure to sustain, in the face of changing patterns of social differentiation, their 'broad church' character; their failure, in the context of Britain's persistent economic decline, to redeem their electoral pledges and meet the aspirations of their erstwhile supporters. In a political climate of considerable scepticism and mistrust, it seems unlikely that the old parties will be able to reduce the volume of contestatory action, unlikely that they will succeed in channelling discontent or ambition back into the old moulds.

Urban politics: issues old and new

Recently there has been much interest in urban politics.[23] The 'new' urban sociology of the 1970s led to vigorous debate about the role of cities and their regions within the highly integrated and centralized economies and polities of contemporary western states and out of this came a renewed concern with the struggles for power which took place at a local level. Many writers reminded us that it was through local agencies that national decisions concerning welfare provision, housing, transport, educaton and medical services were implemented. This did not necessarily mean that local authorities were mere unresponsive agents, blindly doing the bidding of those in Westminster or Whitehall, but it did mean that to assess the working out of government policies we would need to explore the politics of the municipalities and regions in some detail.

The expansion of local government activities along with the effects of inflation (bearing both on local authority wage bills and interest charges) has strained the traditional relationships between central and local administrations. Since the mid-1970s governments at Westminster have sought to reduce the proportion of local current expenditure borne by central government, an understandable concern when one realises that in 1975–6 this amounted to 67.3 per cent. The efforts to curb local authority spending and to give to the central government more directive capacity were redoubled once the Conservative Party under Margaret Thatcher was elected and led to even sharper confrontations between the two levels of administration. A number of local authorities tried to resist the policy of selling council houses: Dundee, for instance, maintained a vigorous opposition on this throughout the first two years of Tory rule. Elsewhere, in Lambeth and Lothian, councillors committed themselves to the defence of their budgets and their services and only yielded to the central government after long and bitter campaigns and the threat of enactment or legislation strengthening the hand of the Minister of the Environment or the Secretary of State for Scotland.

The relationship, then, between central government and the local authorities is neither simple nor static. The renewed study of urban politics encourages us to explore it in much more detail.

Contemporary writing in urban sociology has focused attention on the role of local authorities[24] or the local offices of government agencies partly because there has been a good deal of popular agitation about their policies and practices. In the study of power and conflict these are clearly very important. After all, these are institutions that people confront in their everyday lives; these are bodies whose decisions affect them and these are structures they can hope to change. Thus, local councillors, local government officials, administrators of the local health and social security bureaucracies – these became the targets of the lobbyists, the petitioners and the demonstrators. And what they are concerned about, in many instances, is the distribution and control of the vast public property – the urban infrastructure, the systems of transport or housing or education – that have grown up in the past thirty-five years. But these are not the only reasons why the study of urban politics has been high on the agenda. A much more substantial factor can be found in the theoretical interest in the role of the state, including the 'local state' among many who write on urban affairs. Although authors of all persuasions have seen the increasing role of the state as a major feature of modern capitalist societies, it has been the Marxian commentators who have done most to press the 'problem' of the state to the centre of our concerns. Their interests revolve principally around the issue of just how the activities of the state contribute to the maintenance of capitalism by underwriting many of the costs of the economic infrastructure or by providing housing, education and health care and thereby assisting the 'reproduction of the labour force'. In an extremely lucid and perceptive account of the several strands of writing which address these issues, Saunders proposes that it is possible to distil from the debates a fundamental distinction between 'social investment' and 'social consumption' to refer to the state's expenditure, first, on those items that support or facilitate production, and second, on those that constitute investment in the reproduction of labour power.[25] His examination of the debates about the role of the modern state and its impact on local authorities leads him back to the issue raised by Castells more than a decade ago: [26] the problem of defining the proper, the theoretically defensible concerns of urban sociology. Saunders argues that urban sociology should be concerned above all with the process of 'social consumption', with the provisions that support the working population, and with the kinds of competitive struggles that develop around these. He suggests that social investment functions have generally been removed from local government and that struggles over basic economic policies are these days located at the national level and are resolved partly through class-based politics and partly (and increasingly) through 'corporate' politics where organized labour and big business are directly involved in policy-making.

The effect of defining the proper concerns of urban sociology in this way is rather curious in that it seems to attach such overwhelming importance to the matter of state intervention and manages to banish class politics from the realm of local struggles. It is not a view which we share, for it seems to us that in the cities and the regions of the country, political action, using the term very broadly, is addressed to matters of social investment as well as to those of consumption, and that alongside those there persist many other conflicts over the rights, privileges and power of private capital. The state may well be more important nowadays, but this should surely not lead us to play down the signifiance of private property, both in industry and real estate. This keeps alive the politics of class at a local level.

The politics of class revolves as always around forms of property from which groups and individuals derive material and symbolic benefits. In a society where the state intervenes in so many ways, the relationships formed around diverse property interests are frequently modified, moulded, channelled by public agencies. Thus, the politics of class is generally about much more than a straightforward confrontation between superior and subordinate classes meeting head on. Saunders and others are right when they insist that class relations are not bounded by local markets or local polities. Classes are national formations (indeed, international these days) and the principal struggles are conducted on the stage of national politics, but *local* class struggles still go on and they matter. The importance of class conflicts are seen most clearly if we think of single-industry towns (still common enough in newer societies like Canada or Australia, even if they are relatively scarce in Britain). In such places the owners and the managers often face the workers in a relatively direct way. Far more towns and cities are dependent upon a small array of large employers, most of whom, let us say, are not directly represented on the council. None the less, it is a safe bet that much council business will be informed by the interests, the divergent interests, of workers and employers. Such interests become very clear at times of recession when a plant closes down and when new business has to be attracted. Perhaps the most obvious way of illustrating the survival of class politics is to point to the ways in which *rentiers* and others involved in property dealing feature as members of councils or can be shown to have extensive connections with local politicians. The relationship between the developers and those whose homes and livelihoods they threaten or control, are *class* relationships. As we argued in the previous chapter, traditional landlordism may have declined in the United Kingdom but the power of corporate developers has greatly increased. Urban property is used by many of those who have it as a productive resource.

The case, though, can be argued on even broader grounds. For Weber, a class consisted of those who occupied a similar market situation. On that basis, they constituted a potential, a 'quasi-group'. In practice, real social groups formed within the major boundaries of the 'class dimension'; networks of social contact arose among those enjoying similar locations and similar prospects and experience of mobility. These constituted what Weber called 'social' classes. It is these social classes, especially in their local manifestations that form important bases for political mobilization. they form associations – parties – to represent their material interests, their capacities for reproduction and their status.

In local politics, if we judge by the pamphlets and the speeches, the electoral battles are often conducted in the language of 'class'. Is this mere rhetoric? We think not, for though the local authorities (or local agencies of central government) have limited capacities to alter the economic circumstances of the citizens, still we cannot portray them as totally impotent. They can and do seek to exercise some control over the character and distribution of employment and of economic opportunities. Moreover, since the 1960s they have become major employers in their own right as well as the providers of numerous contracts. It is worth remembering that many of the first 'labour' councillors involved themselves in local government in order to represent council employees. Today the 'politics of class' requires us to look even more closely at public authorities as employers, because today they shape directly and indirectly the livelihooods of thousands of manual workers, white-collar workers, teachers, diverse professionals and a good many business people.

So, class politics cannot be wished away. But that is not to deny that the salience of class conflict at local levels has been reduced. Today there are new bases for political action. In a recent article, Dunleavy develops the idea of conflict arising from 'consumption sectors'.[27] He tries to show how the the declining association between occupational class and political alignment in Britain may be explained in terms of consumption interests. Most importantly, he forces us to think about the position of groups and individuals with respect to state intervention in the provision of resources like houses, roads and schools. Access to and perception of state subsidies, he suggests, mould political attitudes and structure conflict. As state intervention in the processes of consumption grows, so different 'locations' with regard to important items like houses or transport become the bases for political action. And specifically political action is appropriate because *collective* consumption is so evidently shaped by politicians and administrators. For more than ten years now many writers have been stressing the importance of collective consumption issues, and in much of the Marxian material there is the suggestion that the collective organizations forged to contest the distribution of public resources – 'the trades unions of consumption', as Castells calls them – will bring together some who, in class terms, are unlikely bedfellows. There is certainly some truth in this, but few sociologists or political scientists in Britain would see here the prospect of the widespread and radical mobilization some continental writers claimed to see in France and Italy.[28]

However, it does seem reasonable to argue that as the importance of consumption issues has risen, so the salience of class interests rooted in the production system has receded and support for those political parties that grew out of the long-established class divisions has become less coherent and predictable. Moreover, recognition of *class* interests is impeded by the relatively rapid changes in the occupational structure and the apparent diversification of the two big blocs of 'middle class' and 'working class'. In these circumstances, much conflict becomes 'de-institutionalized'; traditional agencies of representation – not just the political parties – are bypassed in the search for novel means of political expression. Inevitably this means that much of the action is sporadic, many of the associations ephemeral or schismatic. But the climate of doubt and criticism, the availability of ideologies stressing the need for participation and political innovation ensures easy regeneration of grass-roots political activity. This is to argue for the decline but not the death of the politics of class in the city.

One way of interpreting much of the urban discontent today is to see it as a response to a new kind of dependency – to what Touraine likes to call 'alienation'.[29] It is a response to the sense of impotence felt by many people when confronted by the legislators and admini- strators, by the complex rules and procedures of large public bureaucracies. The citizens try to influence their political representa- tives and check the power of the full-time officials but, having learned how easily they can be fobbed off by the experts and the manipulators, or how insidious are the processes of incorporation,[30] they resort more frequently to protest rather than to participation, to defiance rather than accommodation.

Touraine's vision of a post-industrial society is one in which domination by experts – technocrats and bureaucrats – is a real threat and although he can be accused of overemphasizing the importance of 'knowledge' as opposed to 'capital' and of neglecting the still fundamental *industrial* character of modern western societies, none the less his analysis touches upon some important and real changes. Many people clearly do feel threatened by the complex systems of government and administration. What they come to understand through their daily experiences is how varied and extensive are the powers centred in the town halls and the local governmental agencies. These powers rest on several things.

First, and most obviously, on the capacity to shape the flow of goods and services, to determine, within limits, who shall benefit from municipal largesse. This is 'material' power. Often, indeed mostly, their discretionary powers favour the dominant economic interests in an area, but the pattern is not invariable; there is nothing inevitable about this. It is contingent upon the precise political and economic structure in which they are embedded. Just as significantly, for our purpose, routine disposition of resources puts these members of the 'service' stratum in a position where, through a good deal of 'bargaining' with the politicians, they can utilize public funds to foster the growth of positions to be filled by others like themselves. And, at this point, we should be careful not to confine ourselves to local government officials, for alongside the regular bureaucracies there have emerged a whole host of new 'authorities' – the so-called quangos – whose actions and decisions are subject to extremely weak forms of accountability. If, at all levels, the ranks of the bureaucrats have grown, that is in some measure the result of their skill, their effectiveness in extending the scope of their various bureaux, adding research capabilities to their administrative tasks and generally proliferating the hierarchies of office. We are not talking here of some trivial processes of featherbedding individual careers; what is at stake is the growth and regeneration of a stratum. Bureaucrats in town halls, officials in welfare agencies and the health service have skilfully used the 'model' of the traditional professions to win for themselves a considerable autonomy, a capacity to sustain and recreate these occupational niches.

Second, the power of those who have some control over collective resources rests on moral force. In their day-to-day operations, the government officials and their administrators establish moral conventions, customary rules (which often extend their legally established authority). The moral conventions serve to define eligibility, to govern the queuing for scarce public resources. In some areas – in many parts of Scotland, for instance – the scale of public provision is so vast and the prospect of democratic control or accountability is so slim that many of the poorest groups in the population are forced into an abject dependency on those who manage public property.

Finally, some of those who control the items of collective consumption, and especially those who help shape the urban environment are engaged in processes of cultural domination. Planners, architects and others are in the business of manipulating symbolic and cultural life. They manipulate the cultural life of the working class when they plan the 'renewal' of old inner-city districts, changing the physical environment in ways which inhibit old patterns of sociability, and controlling the admission of leisure and recreational resources in the 'renewed' environment according to their own criteria of desirability.

The cultural force of these members of the 'service class' is perhaps most evident when we consider how public bodies determine the content of education, give grants and subsidies to approved art forms and generally mould the cultural environment. Increasingly the canons of approval or disapprobation are established not by the bourgeoisie but by a bureaucratised intelligentsia.

Many of the struggles – from the orderly presentation of views by a council sponsored tenants' association to the strident demands of a protest group – are attempts to establish or re-establish a measure of popular control or to resist threats to personal and group identity. Homes, neighbourhoods, schools, local places of entertainment have always contributed to an individual's sense of identity and security but to the extent that work for many people in a contemporary industrial society becomes less absorbing of energies and commitments, to the extent that position in the systems of consumption becomes more important, so they acquire greater significance.

For most people in Britain, the network of social contacts, the groups and associations in which they most regularly participate, the places in which they meet and spend their leisure are mainly local; the boundaries of their social and cultural life are to a large extent given by their town and the district they live in. The resources on which they depend for the creation of their social life are therefore mainly local. Not surprisingly then, people fight to defend resources like schools, shopping areas, pubs and places of recreation which are subject to manipulation and sometimes to destruction at the behest of public agencies.

At the very moment where non-work life has become more extensive for families and individuals, the capacity for political and bureaucratic manipulation of these elements has greatly increased. The politics of consumption seems to be about three things: about justice in the allocation of resources, about security and identity, and perhaps as a by-product, about the renewal of public life in the city. These are the objects of the new struggles. In the last decade or so in Britain, we have seen rent strikes and squatting campaigns; innumerable community action groups, residents' and tenants' associations involved mostly in negotiations but sometimes in defiant confrontations with planners and politicians; groups formed to oppose transport plans, to protect the environment, to oppose or to urge industrial development, to contest educational changes and a host of other manifestations of discontent.[31] Most of the associations are short-lived: most are fairly specific in their objectives. But in some instances, they have endured over several years and greatly expanded their range of concerns. One or two have become so institutionalized that they have attracted money from the EEC (and aroused the jealousy of established political bodies and elected representatives in doing so). Even the most durable associations on the monolithic housing estates offer only a poor substitute for the bonds of neighbourhood, kinship and community that characterized some of the old working-class areas. But they do in a few cases seem to have produced a new pride, sense of dignity and confidence in local populations. Where they combine recreational, cultural and social activity with serious economic programmes and political campaigns, they offer some hope for the regeneration of locally based collective life.

The growth of the welfare state has meant the growth, on a massive scale, of locally administered urban resources. The spread of this kind of collectivism carries with it inherent dangers as well as evident and most important blessings. Over the past decade or so the benefits have attracted rather less attention than the shortcomings. The proliferation of pressure groups and protest organisations in the cities seems to signal recognition of the negative aspect that Harrington refers to when he comments that the development of collectivism could go in one or two directions:

> On the one extreme, there could be an authoritarian, or totalitarian collectivism run by a bureaucratic class; on the other, there could be a domestic communitarianism with considerable decentralisation and self-management.[32]

Much of the 'new' politics in the city is surely about resisting the former and attaining the latter. Popular protest, aggressive, innovative, disrespectful forms of political action are essential to contest both the persistent power of private property and the emergent power of those who manipulate the new public property. And that is recognized most clearly perhaps by 'dissidents' from the ranks of the bureaucratised professionals, those planners, lawyers and educators who can so readily be found at the head of the parades, leading or advising the protestors.

If the cities today are 'noisy' places that is not to regretted, not to be compared adversely to the consensus, the relative tranquility of some imagined time past. Rather it is to be welcomed, for that combination of political cynicism and political competence[33] now so pervasive among the relatively young is probably our best safeguard against the worst excesses of capitalistic profiteering, against the threats of bureaucratic domination and our best hope for some renewal of public life in our cities.

Chapter 7

An Agenda for Research

At the end, let's go back to the beginning and ask what implications our approach has for research. We began by criticizing structuralist Marxism, finding it too deterministic, too arcane and frequently too concerned to promote theorizing in preference to detailed enquiry. Since we wrote that chapter the Urban and Regional Research group of the International Sociological Association, the group which has done so much to promote the 'new urban sociology' has had a new agenda written for its 1982 World Congress deliberations by Ivan Szelenyi.[1] He provides a cool appraisal of the strengths and weaknesses of the structuralist strand which dominated the work of this group; he outlines areas of enquiry neglected by this approach and sketches recent economic and political developments which require attention. There is much in his critique of structuralism which echoes our own misgivings: the concern that such an approach was often blinkered and failed to acknowledge the salience of conflicts which could not be reduced to 'class struggle', or failed to see that government actions did not always or inevitably reproduce the 'capitalist relations of production'. Moreover, he finds structuralist Marxism in urban research to have been somewhat ethnocentric, focusing our attention too exclusively on the cities of the advanced industrial societies of the west and promoting too little curiosity about third-world urbanisation or the experience of urban development within the socialist states of eastern Europe.

We find ourselves in accord not only with much of the criticism, but much more importantly, with several of his proposals for research. Szelenyi writes as a committed democratic socialist, one who has direct practical experience of living in a socialist state observing and researching social developments there, but his socialism, his Marxism, lacks the dogmatic certainty of the structuralists. The programme of investigation he enjoins admits a degree of theoretical diversity which will encourage convergence of research, with Marxists and non-Marxists engaged in an open dialogue. That is surely to be welcomed. If, as seems to be happening, urban sociologists can set for themselves a more permissive, humanistic and practical agenda, then the next decade of the 'new urban' sociology could be exciting indeed.

In this little book we have tried to explore some of the ways in which themes from Max Weber can be used to complement the dominant perspective within the 'new' urban sociology, so we should now ask how this might inform a programme of research. We can start with some very broad points.

First, it must be stressed that we need much more *empirical* research. In the past ten years much effort has been devoted to 'theorizing' about urban matters because, as the structuralists insisted, much of the traditional work was mere empiricism; 'facts' were gathered it seemed for their own sake, or for some unexamined policy purposes and over a long period this had divorced most urban sociology from the main theoretical currents in the discipline. There was truth in this, but as often happens with academic fashions, the determination to redress the imbalance between theory and empirical enquiry meant that the pendulum was pushed so hard toward the 'theoretical' pole that empirical investigations, especially those using any of the 'harder' techniques, fell into disfavour.[2] As a result, many important changes in our cities took place almost unobserved. For example, there have been, as we tried to indicate in our chapter on market forces, important changes in the nature of the property markets in Britain, the source of capital and property investment, the nature of the development companies, the roles of governments: all these have altered. Since much importance is attached to 'property capital' in Marxist writings on the city, it is astonishing that we have to turn so often to journalists rather than sociologists for information on all this. And one could make similar remarks about the lack of sociological research on the building industry. More broadly, we seem mainly reliant on official statistical sources or other government documents for knowledge of changing industrial, occupational and social structures in particular cities and regions. There are only a few attempts by urban sociologists in Britain to explore major structural changes in our cities in a detailed, firsthand and critical way. Then again, in the mid-1970s we had, first in England and Wales, then in

Scotland, major alterations to the systems of local government, but specifically sociological investigations of an event that has considerable theoretical interest (given all the debates about a Marxist theory of the state) are hard to find.

To argue, as we would, that there is now an urgent need for much more empirical research is not to denigrate the efforts of those who saw the need for theory, nor to call for a new wave of empiricism. It is to say that in sociology our theoretical achievements are extremely modest and that in our view we shall move toward better conceptual frameworks and general understanding only if we retain a healthy interdependence between theory building and observation of the 'world out there'. But more than that, the need for empirical investigation is now of paramount importance if we are to offset, even partially, the deliberate reduction of research carried out by government departments and other agencies. The investigative capacities of the Office of Population Censuses and Surveys and of the Home Office Research Unit are to be reduced. The Centre for Environmental Studies and the Personal Social Services Council have been closed and many other units producing social and economic data are to be wound up or restricted. As Peter Townsend observes:

> The Government's actions are, in effect, a direct restriction on democratic rights. In the guise of cutting manpower and saving money, the Government's proposals seem designed to divert, contain and reduce criticisms of government policies.[3]

The government's policies for our cities and the secular changes taking place within them require, in a democratic society, close and constant surveillance. Within the very limited resources now available for research, we need to give priority to empirical investigations of what is going on in our urban areas.

The nature of our empirical enquiries needs to be varied. Alongside the researches which document and analyse structural changes we also need sensitive examination of the everyday lives of social groups within the cities. There is a need still for good urban ethnography which can provide a basis for understanding the prejudices and predelictions, the hopes and fears of our urban populations. We need to be able to grasp and comprehend social action especially the collective actions of, say, youngsters on the dole, immigrants in the inner city or our aged citizens. The matter of consciousness has relevance to more than just the study of class conflict. As we have seen all too clearly in recent months, politicians and journalists are very quick to impute motives to those who riot or demonstrate. Urban sociologists should be in a position to offer something better than these often glib suppositions.

A second general requirement of our urban research is that it should be *historically informed,* sensitive to the processes that have shaped urban institutions, urban environments and the ideologies and actions of particular social groups. We need historical awareness because our task is to explore change and conflict and cohesion in the city. It is essential, when considering institutions – the frameworks of local government or the health or housing or welfare agencies – to appreciate that the liberties or rights that they confer have been won by struggle. They were not bestowed by benevolent rulers but ceded gradually and grudgingly by local and national elites confronted by sections of the citizenry anxious to secure for themselves some say in decision-making, some improvement in their material circumstances, some basis for fuller citizenship. How those institutions and agencies work, how they respond to citizens and clients is much affected by the particular histories of these agencies for they are, as Friedland, Piven and Alford put it, 'repositories of historical demands'.[4] The practices and procedures with which they operate, the commitments which they acknowledge are the outcome of prior struggles. Current efforts to extend or alter them are constrained by those legacies.

It is also clear that rights and liberties, once secured, need constant vigilance if they are to be retained, for established elites and rising strata, those who rule and manage our cities and society are quick to appropriate those items which are not securely held. E. P. Thompson, in his essay on 'The State of the Nation', conveys brilliantly the insidious processes whereby traditional rules and practices, once vigorously fought for, can be reclaimed by ruling elites.[5] Though he is mainly concerned with these matters on a national level the effects of the changes are sharply felt (and indeed often have their origins in) local struggles. For instance, Thompson has argued – and recent events give credence to his view – that the police in Britain are not always subject to proper democratic control, that in some instances they have usurped the role of the civil authorities in matters of public order. No one reading the race relations literature over the past decade or following the debates surrounding the 1981 riots in the English cities, can fail to observe the growth of police powers, or the deep concern among immigrants or among the youth of the inner city about the methods of policing and about the accountability of the police. The role and specific actions of the Special Patrol Group, the death of Blair Peach apparently from a truncheon blow, the smashing of shops and houses by police officers in the aftermath of the Brixton riots – all these matters raise profound doubts about the role of police and the maintenance of public order in particular cities, but beyond that they raise matters of the greatest constitutional importance if, as Thompson believes, they are merely one part of a much wider process whereby our political culture is being changed.

History teaches us then that precious liberties, vital democratic practices have constantly to be defended. Sociological studies of struggles for domination, the nature of social conflict, of public order and political culture at local levels can play a valuable part in this, alerting us to changes in institutions in which we have some interest, and about which we may have some say. The defence of democratic practices, or the extension of democracy requires local action, for as students of social movements have often pointed out, it is the local institutions to which ordinary people have access.[6] For most of us the chance of altering things on a national level seems remote, but within our neighbourhoods or cities, in the town halls and regional councils there is some hope that we can, collectively, be active and creative.

Because it is historically informed, the social movements' literature also gives a perspective on recent unrest in our cities which suggests that the level of violence is by no means unprecedented, that the image of British cities as 'normally' peaceable places patrolled only by avuncular constables is a comforting myth but one which will not stand much historical or sociological scrutiny. An historical approach helps us 'relativise' these recent manifestations of discontent. It enables us also to recognize that modes of political expression reflect the structural location of different groups – those who feel themselves to be excluded from more peaceable means take their troubles on to the streets – and to appreciate that repertoires of protest are historically conditioned by the cultural histories of particular groups of actors.[7] Above all it reminds us that direct popular action has often been the means whereby rights and liberties were established and defended. We should beware of accepting the 'official' designation of popular disturbances as 'anarchic' and 'destructive' and look very critically upon the extensions of central and police powers in the name of 'law and order'. This is not to justify or glorify violence and looting:

there is nothing democratic about burning buildings or policemen. But it is to say that we need to look very carefully at the material and political processes that affect the communities where riots break out and to look with equal care at the responses to the violence.

Thus, what we are recommending is not simply the tying of sociology to conventional history. Rather what we need is an historical dimension to our sociological imagination so that we see how both structures and actions are set in time and that what has gone before leaves residues of procedures, codes, practices and responses.

Historical sensitivity gives us a base for comparison of a temporal kind but we also require as our third general feature of urban research a broader comparative approach. We need to explore much more fully than we have done under the auspices of Marxian structuralism the processes which help shape and interrelate cities across regions, countries and continents. Certainly we need more investigation of third-world urbanization and the ways in which it is linked to and dependent upon the development of international capitalism *and* international socialism. Already we have some excellent studies, especially on Latin American cities[8] but also of India and Africa[9] which attempt to show the impact of western capitalism on third-world settlements. But as Szelenyi reminds us, there are alternatives to capitalist development, and socialist experiments in eastern Europe (which are rooted in traditions of urban life distinct from those of Italy or France or Britain)[10] deserve attention too, as do those in third-world countries which draw their inspiration from socialist 'models'. Distinct patterns of urban development can be found within single countries, as, for instance, in the contemporary and historical contrasts between Scottish cities and their English and Welsh counterparts. Even contradictory forms of development seem able to coexist – as in Tanzania where an economic and social structure which draws much of its inspiration from socialist sources is none the less establishing its new capital, Dodoma, according to precepts established by planners experienced in creating 'corporate' cities in Canada.

The patterns of urban development in those parts of the industrial capitalist world where economic expansion and rapid urbanization have been taking place also need our attention. City growth in Canada and Australia, for instance,[11] is a phenomenon which demands a broad comparative approach. Much of the recent growth

– and often it has been spectacular in its speed and opulence – depends upon the movement of people, of corporations and capital from western Europe and the USA to these 'new' territories. In these countries the imprint of corporate capitalism is sharper, clearer, less modified by earlier phases of economic development than one finds in Europe or indeed in much of the USA. They provide excellent 'laboratories' for exploring such things as the relationship between corporations and the political powers of the municipalities and the state, or the role played by property companies and traditional landed interests from Europe in the rapid and very profitable urbanization which distinguishes their latest phases of development.

Finally, we require studies of groups of cities, not just case studies of single centres but sociological work which might complement the efforts of geographers and urban historians to explore the hierarchies of cities within particular regions or countries. Though it takes a good many years for a city to change its character radically, we should try to look at the processes of flux: the broad trends of rising power and prosperity on the one hand, or the slide into economic or political subordination on the other. In Britain we know all too well that some cities, like Glasgow, have been faced with decline in their manufacturing bases for many years now, others which were thought relatively secure in their prosperity, like Birmingham, have only recently felt the impact of economic decline.

In their recent book, *The Good City*, Donnison and Soto[12] provide evidence of the considerable diversity among British cities, a diversity which greatly differentiates the opportunities, the life chances of individuals and of groups living in them. They suggest that in order to understand what makes for a 'good' city we must ask what factors 'create a power structure or "polity" which is likely to protect potentially vulnerable people' and what 'provides both good opportunites for the less skilled and more vulnerable, and a distribution of opportunites between socio-economic groups which is not too unequal'.[13] The way to do this, they argue is to foster research, which examines the patterns of investment in industry and housing, and in the interactions between the markets for jobs, houses, schools, health care and other services not just in single settlements but in whole systems of cities.

In our future research we need to follow up some of Donnison's and Soto's recommendations. We need to go beyond the statistical profiles and look more closely at the *processes* which promote improvements in material conditions, in the distribution of cultural goods and the capacities for political engagement and local democracy. And in doing this we must accord much greater significance to the political dimension; we must see cities as local polities, polities set in a wider complex of domination.

Beyond these very general prescriptions though, we can identify four particular themes which ought to be central to our research efforts.

First we need to recognize that our 'urban economies' like our national ones are highly variegated and that we must provide a *sociography of the plural economy*. Conceptions of the diversity of economic relationships and modes of production seem as yet to be very fluid. There is no general agreement as to how we should identify the quite different ways by which capital is raised, work is organized and livings earned, but there is emerging a broad agreement that in Britain, say, we are are dealing with something much more complex than 'the capitalist mode of production'. It has long been recognized that alongside or perhaps, beneath, the regular structure of economic relationships there exist a great many ways by which people secure a livelihood and accomplish work. There are many men and women who supplement their regular wages or salaries by 'moonlighting' – taking on extra jobs in the evenings or the weekends. Goods and services are exchanged in various bartering arrangements[14] and many have discovered the benefits of simply working on their own account in an 'unofficial' way. Sociologists have also recognized, somewhat belatedly, the contribution of domestic work to our overall economy, and have begun to explore the range of economic activity carried out, mainly by women, in the home. Thus, we find terms like 'the informal', 'the black' or 'the domestic' economy being used with increasing frequency. Or, drawing from the Marxian tradition, the recognition of the coexistence in the cities of the west of 'pre-capitalist modes of production' of 'petty commodity production', of 'domestic modes of production' or of a 'state mode of production'.[15]

Our appreciation of this diversity has been sharpened by the dramatic economic decline in Britain in the last few years, for as employment prospects in the 'formal' economy diminish, so more and more people turn to other ways of eking out a living. But even before the latest downturn in the economies of the west it was obvious that in order to avoid high taxes or government regulation, a large number of transactions were being carried on in a kind of subterranean economy. Visitors to Sweden, for instance, often learned that there were many devious ways by which citizens of that country shielded themselves from the tax inspector's gaze. Recently economists have begun to treat the 'informal' economy much more seriously – and greatly inflate their estimates of its size.[16] In their article, 'Work Outside Employment: Some Preliminary Speculations',[17] which stands as a prolegomenon to their research on this topic, Gershuny and Pahl outline some of the main reasons for the decline in regular employment – the fact that productivity is rising faster than demand for manufactured goods, that the service sector can no longer absorb labour displaced from manufacturing – and they go on to discuss the various adaptations to this. Like most writers on this matter, they foresee the growth of the informal economy in which goods and services are produced at home or with the assistance of friends, neighbours or kin and the growth too of a 'black' economy where production and trade take place outside the systems of public regulation and taxation. In our cities, especially those with very high levels of unemployment, it may be that these alternative economies will develop on a considerable scale, that some of our urban centres will contan large numbers for whom backyard production and back-street trading afford some prospects for acquiring new skills or greater autonomy, or in a gloomier vein, the only ways of rising above the level of the dole payments. If that happens, we may find ourselves looking at our own manifestation of the dual economy so vividly captured in Bryan Roberts's descriptions of Latin American cities.[18]

To understand these changes, we shall find ourselves looking at the restructuring of capitalism: at the ways in which new technology makes possible unprecedented levels of output with very much smaller workforces, at the deliberate movement of much manufacturing activity to the countries of the third world. Many multinational corporations are shifting their operations to regions where large pools of cheap labour exist, where authoritarian regimes guarantee, at least for some while, the docility of the labour force or where traditional cultures, especially in the Orient, provide a commitment to work or to the firm which in some ways substitute for the protestant ethic of the west. Close to home, we shall find ourselves examining the activities of the state and those policies, which deliberately or unintentionally, encourage the relocation of much industry away from the major cities with their high costs or, as is often the case in the inner-city areas, their relatively unskilled labour forces. In all events, we shall need to develop an awareness of the ultimate connections between political decisions, political structures and the lineaments of these 'plural economies'. An appreciation of 'political economy' is a prerequisite for our analysis.

In Britain, the importance of the political dimension is surely very obvious. The second main theme of our research enterprise must be the description and explanation of *the ways in which the 'New Right' gained power and sought to shape our cities* (and a parallel undertaking will be needed in the USA). The policies of the Thatcher government have represented a substantial break with the ideals shaping British society since the Second World war and in the cities we have been able to observe the Conservatives' efforts to reassert an old pattern of domination, one in which the prerogatives of employers are to be restored and market forces given freer rein. The rise to power of Margaret Thatcher and her monetarist advisers and colleagues, first in the Tory Party and then as a government, can be traced to the conspicuous failure of Labour and of the 'progressive' Heathite Conservatives to cope with Britain's long-term economic decline, exacerbated as this was by the world recession that followed the dramatic raising of oil prices in 1973. From 1974 until the election of 1979 there was ample evidence of what historians refer to as a *'grand peur'*, an outburst of defensive, fearful behaviour on the part of elite and bourgeois groups whose apocalyptic visions of the 'breakdown of law and order', of 'untramelled union power' stimulated the rise of vigilante groups, so-called freedom associations, middle-class defence leagues and a host of 'politicized' business associations.[19] Mrs Thatcher and her radical Conservatives skilfully orchestrated this discontent, excoriating the unions and the supposedly parasitic bureaucrats, exposing what they saw as the incubus of dangerous leftism in diverse institutions and collective bodies. Their purpose was to restore commitment to and belief in capitalism: as they saw it, a moral system as much as an economic one. To this end, small business became a useful symbol, a representation of the virtues of the independent entrepreneurial life, and at the same time, an alleged means of restoring economic vigour and reducing unemployment.

Once in power, the 'new right' addressed itself without hesitation to the reform of property relations, attempting to reverse those processes which have, over thirty years and more, imposed restrictions and responsibilities on those with economic power. Thus, they sought to restore the prerogatives of those who own business and reduce the power of trades unions.Taxation of the wealthy was relaxed in order, it was said, to encourage investment and profits, while at the same time, unemployment benefits were reduced and supplementary benefits for the very poorest cut back. The policies were, of course, not specifically 'urban' in their construction but the effects on our cities have been very clear. Support for public housing, which for a while enjoyed a good measure of bipartisan agreement, was largely withdrawn. Councils everywhere were enjoined to sell off as much as possible of their public housing stock and to curtail (in practice, virtually to cease) their public housing construction programmes. This was done with very little apparent recognition of the vast differences in the levels of public housing up and down the country or in different parts of our major conurbations. In some Scottish cities where the majority of housing is publicly owned, this policy has had quite different implications from those it has had in small towns in the south-east. At the same time, some planning regulations have been relaxed and diverse forms of public property in our cities 'put on to the market'. Everywhere the effort was to reduce collective, public ownership and to 'privatise' land and real estate. And the quest to increase private enterprise did not stop there. Wherever possible public agencies were encouraged to subcontract some parts of their operations and this affected all the public services delivered through local, that is to say, largely urban administrations. Local health boards were directed to promote private medicine, even in areas where the medical profession had little sympathy for it; private education was boosted at the expense of state education. And failure to comply with the wishes of this new right elicited efforts to increase central control. In England and Wales the Minister for the Environment took measures to punish recalcitrant councils and in Scotland the Secretary of State acquired special powers to reduce the autonomy of local authorities. The effect was greatly to strengthen that tendency, already marked under previous administrations, towards a kind of authoritarian centralism. The pre-election claim that the radical right was intent on 'rolling back the state' and encouraging 'local autonomy' rang hollow indeed.

Our research on the cities must pay attention to these developments. In their attempts to manage Britain's decline, successive governments have been engaged in the quest for greater and greater control of our local institutions, but with the election of the Thatcher government, these efforts were greatly increased. The processes were insidious, their effects almost invariably anti-democratic. The recent outbreaks of rioting in English cities highlighted one very important aspect of this. The response of the Tory Government to popular agitation was to look for ways of strengthening the police, providing them with new technology and legitimating 'positive' action to put down disturbances. In areas where there was already considerable mistrust between the police and the local community, such moves further eroded bonds between constabulary and citizenry. In some inner-city areas and some large council estates the local populations, especially the young among them, have come to view the police with considerable suspicion, whites and blacks alike complaining that they are subject to unwarranted searches and surveillance or that the police are less than even-handed in their treatment of them and unresponsive to their request for assistance. Moves to re-equip the police and to bolster their authority will do nothing to restore the confidence of many in these areas. They will appear simply to strengthen the ties between the police and central authority and further to remove them from local democratic control.

This is not a trivial matter but an important indication of the change which is taking place in our political culture and for sociologists and other social scientists. It indicates that we should not treat the riots of Brixton or Southall or Toxteth as an invitation to conduct yet more surveys of the underprivileged. Rather, we should investigate more carefully the role of those with authority: the politicians at both local and national levels, bureaucratic powers – especially those most closely involved in the discipline and control of the population – and the police. It is easy to scrutinize the lives of the vulnerable; it is difficult, but necessary for us to examine closely and critically those who have responsibility for the maintenance of public order. In our local, urban studies we need research on the growth of 'authoritarian centralism' in all its aspects and on those developments which constitute for the citizens a loss of liberty. It is a loss of liberty if, as a youngster, you are unwilling to leave your house for fear of arrest on 'suspicion'; and that is a reality for both black and white adolescents in some areas. But equally it is a loss of liberty if the level of criminal violence is such that to go out means risking mugging or racial harassment – which fears haunt many of the inhabitants of our more neglected neighbourhoods. The ideas about justice and liberty and the actual experience of these, the aspirations for democratic control and the real engagement in forms of local self-determination – these intensely political themes deserve to be high on our research agenda.

The policies of the new right are concerned with the reimposition of a narrow class rule: a pattern of domination in which the new middle class, the technocrats and bureaucrats of the 'service' class are to be put in their place no less firmly than the manual workers. In seeking to impose that pattern of domination, with all that it implies in terms of the piecemeal demolition of the welfare state, the new right will encounter opposition: opposition from Labour councils, opposition from trades unions, opposition on the streets. The sharpest struggles will come in the cities. Cities will indeed be at the heart of political action; for control over their institutions, their public property and their populations is vital for the success of the new abrasive conservatism. That is why the Minister of the Environment and the Secretary of State for Scotland took extraordinary powers to impose their will upon city councils from Camden to Dundee.

A third item on our research agenda is intimately linked with the foregoing arguments and can be simply stated. We need *to monitor the effects of government policies on the cities*. We need to be able to measure the consequences of all these efforts to 'privatise' our economy. It looks as though we shall be able to depend less and less on official agencies to provide the data, but if we are to sustain any informed political debate, it is vital that we know, for instance, how many council houses have been sold off and what effects the sales will have on local and on national housing markets and housing programmes. Similarly, we should be curious about the offices and retail centres and other assets stripped from the new town corporations and sold to private entrepreneurs. Who buys them? With what long-term intentions? And how does their removal from public ownership affect the lives of local people? Then there is the matter of relaxing planning regulations in order to encourage, it has been said, new building and new industry. How far will the regulations be slackened? Will this really have the desired effects? More specifically, we need to monitor the creation of so-called 'enterprise zones'. The absence of red tape and the lure of rate-free accommodation was intended to attract small businesses, old and new, back into the derelict sites in the inner-city areas, but it seems questionable whether they can fill the premises left vacant by the departing manufacturing companies. Is it possible to create Hong Kong capitalism, as it has been called, in the blackened hearts of English and Scottish cities? Will these developments change in significant ways the local labour markets and, if so, how and with what consequences?

And quite apart from policies like these which bear immediately on the built environment, there are others which deal with employment, education and health. Will the changes in these areas lead to greater opportunites? If so, for whom?

The Thatcher government, more evidently than most, has sought a change not just in material life, not just in the institutional frameworks, but in the moral order. It has sought to win the hearts and minds of men and women, to alter the pattern of their aspirations, curbing collectivist urges and steering ambitions into individualist channels. Can that be done? What are the implications of such an attempt for the nature of the mass media, locally and nationally? And what will happen to dissent? Perhaps Thompson is right to see (and not just under the Tories) an increasingly sophisticated management of consensus and a corresponding segregation of dissent, confining it to *recherché* journals, to odd corners of the universities, but allowing little of it to appear on the television screens or radios or front pages of the newspapers.[20] The stances taken by local media to the struggles against Thatcherite policies deserve to be studied, for they play an important part in the construction, maintenance or undermining of any 'moral orders'. So far, we have paid rather little attention to them. It is not the case that Marxists are uninterested in these 'moral' matters, but an urban sociology which took Weber seriously would certainly have to explore them with considerable care.

Finally, our urban research in the next decade must surely examine the socio-political responses to these efforts of the 'radical right' to alter material and moral frameworks in our cities and regions. In some quarters, of course, there is support for Margaret Thatcher and her policies and it will be important to study those countries or urban areas where they were implemented. This will provide an important part of their overall appraisal. Will they lead to more opportunity, more economic vitality? If so, who will benefit from this?

In many places though, and that means particularly our large cities, there will be a good deal of resistance and already it begins to seem as though there are interesting realignments on the left. In a city like Dundee, with some 60 per cent of its housing stock publicly owned, it was not surprising to find the local Labour administration opposed to the Tory policy of selling off council housing. But as the opposition to this plan has grown, it has revealed a pattern of relations between the council and local unions which seems, for Britain, rather unusual. Over most of the post-war period trades unions in Britain have taken little part in local struggles over housing or other urban issues. To a large degree they have confined themselves to wage-bargaining and to other activities in the sphere of their members' employment. But the 'new right's' efforts to extend private ownership, to curb the power of unions, and its denigration of those who work in the public service – in other words, local government employees and civil servants – has consolidated several oppositional constituencies. It looks as though, in some places, the unions and the local Labour politicians have begun to work closely together and more than that, white-collar and blue-collar unions, NALGO as well as the AUEW, for instance, have joined ranks to oppose the government's plans for housing and for local government finance. Opposition to the new right may well generate a kind of cross-class alliance, a popular local movement spearheaded by a more ideological, self-consciously leftist Labour party. It would be foolish to pretend that at the moment we have more than a few straws in the wind but already the strength and determination of some local councils in their resistance to the new right provide extremely fascinating glimpses of a revitalized local polity. And here we come back to a point of agreement with Szelenyi, for these events suggest that we would do well to look, within these areas of opposition, at a whole series of experiments in local democracy, a series of small-scale but not necessarily trivial attempts to create new ways for people to participate in the shaping of their environments, their schools, and through collective and collaborative efforts born of unemployment, their work lives. As Szelenyi recognizes, *within* capitalist societies there exist glimmerings of a more democratic, a more socialist way of ordering our lives. With three million unemployed in Britain, it would be remarkable indeed if alternative modes of social organisation were not to grow up in opposition to conventional economic and political relations. Thus, we must observe the responses both to the general economic decline and to the policies of this government in particular.

Today in Britain (and in America, and perhaps most western countries) the movement towards a more authoritarian state is accelerating. In this country, the failure of successive governments to restore the nation to anything like economic health produces circumstances of grotesque inequality and much disillusionment with the existing major party machines. In an atmosphere of despair some turn to neo- or crypto-fascist ideas, believing that blacks and Jews can be blamed for our ills and urging upon what seem like increasingly sympathetic governments the need for stronger central control: water cannon for the police, an expanded role for the army, more powers of surveillance, tougher immigration laws to keep out the foreigners.

In these circumstances, we have an urgent need of a sociology which remains true to its original promise as a critical discipline, one that can perform for ordinary men and women (and not just a narrow academic elite) a means of clarifying and demystifying the historical processes in which, as individuals, they are caught up. It needs to be a discipline which can blend structural arguments with an appreciation of subjectivity, one that can meaningfully link public issues with private concerns. To do this, it must combine argument with evidence, theory with practice and it must not disdain the messy task of recommending policies whereby people can reassert their democratic impulses.

The cities, the places where most of us live, are now more than ever at the centre of the struggles for domination; the struggles for supremacy by particular groups and particular ideals. That makes them good places in which to begin.

Notes and References

Introduction

1. Tom Burns, 'Sociological Explanation', in D. Emmet and A. MacIntyre (eds) *Sociological Theory and Philosophical Analysis* (London: Macmillan, 1970).

Chapter 1

1. The most important works are: H. Lefebvre, *La Révolution Urbaine* (Paris: Gallimard, 1970) and *La Pensée Marxiste et la Ville* (Paris: Castermann, 1972); M. Castells, *La Question Urbaine* (London: Edward Arnold, 1976), M. Castells and F. Godard, *Monopolville* (Paris: Mouton, 1974) and M. Castells, *City, Class and Power* (London: Macmillan, 1978); J. Lojkine, 'Contribution to a Marxist Theory of Capitalist Urbanization', pp.119–46 in C. Pickvance (ed.), *Urban Sociology: Critical Essays* (London: Tavistock, 1976); L. Althusser, *For Marx* (New York: Vintage Books, 1970); L. Althusser and E. Balibar, *Reading 'Capital'* (London: New Left Books, 1970).
2. See, for example, M. Harloe (ed.), *Proceedings of the Conference on Urban Change and Conflict* (London: Centre for Environmental Studies, 1975).
3. M. Castells, 'Theory and Ideology in Urban Sociology', in Pickvance, *Urban Sociology*, pp. 60–84
4. Ibid, p. 70.
5. For commentary on the influence of this particular strain of Marxism in urban geography see D. Ley, 'Social Geography and Social Action', pp. 41–57 in D. Ley and M. Samuels (eds), *Humanistic Geography: Prospects and Problems* (Chicago: Maaroufa Press, 1978), and the much more extensive work in preparation – D. Ley and J. Duncan, 'Structural Marxism and the Geography of Advanced Societies: Critical Assessment', Department of Geography, University of British Columbia, July 1980.
6. Such a view has been elegantly developed by F. Braudel in his celebrated *Capitalism and Material Life 1400–1800* (Glasgow: Fontana, 1973) and, among recent studies of early modern towns, C. Friedrichs, *Urban Society in an Age of War: Nördlingen 1580–1720* (Princeton University Press, 1979) provides an instructive account of capitalist growth, class struggle and attendant structural changes in one German centre. J. Foster, *Class Struggle and the Industrial Revolution* (London: Methuen, 1977),

Benwell Community Project, *The Making of a Ruling Class* (Newcastle: Benwell CDP Publications, 1978) and J. Melling, *Housing, Social Policy and the State* (London: Croom Helm, 1980), are also worth consulting.

7. An excellent recent study is B. Roberts, *Cities of Peasants* (London: Edward Arnold, 1978).

8. J. Lojkine, 'A Marxist Theory of Capitalist Urbanization' in Pickvance, *Urban Sociology*, p. 145.

9. The point is made in several places but the clearest expression is found in this article, 'City, Class and Power', in his book of the same title.

10. Inadequacies in his conception of collective consumption are pointed out by Pahl in his article, 'Castells and Collective Consumption', *Sociology*, 12 (2), 1978, pp. 309–15.

11. See the well-known debate between Poulantzas and Miliband: N. Poultanzas, 'The Problem of the Capitalist State', *New Left Review*, 58, 1969, pp. 67–78 and R. Miliband, *New Left Review*, 159, 1970, pp. 53–60. But see too the criticism of the structuralist view of the state contained in E. P. Thompson, *The Poverty of Theory* (London: Merlin Press, 1978) and J. Foster, 'How Imperial London Preserved its Slums', *International Journal of Urban and Regional Research*, 3 (1), 1979, p. 111.

12. C. Cockburn, *The Local State* (London: Pluto Press, 1977).

13. See Castells's account of urban social movements in Spain, 'Urban Social Movements and the Struggle for Democracy', *International Journal of Urban and Regional Research*, 2 (1), 1978, pp. 133–46, or his chapter, 'The Social Prerequisites for the Upheaval of Urban Social Movements', in his *City, Class and Power*, pp. 126–51; and J. Olives, 'The Struggle against Urban Renewal in the Cite d'Aliarté', in Pickvance, *Urban Sociology*, pp. 174–97.

14. R. Pahl, *Whose City?* (Harmondsworth: Penguin, 1975), p. 273, and S. M. Miller, 'Economic Crisis and Oppositional Movements in the USA', *International Journal of Urban and Regional Research*, 1 (1), 1977, pp. 126–31.

15. See P. Leonard (ed.) 'The Sociology of Community Action', *Sociological Review Monograph*, 21, 1975.

16. D. Harvey, *Social Justice and the City* (London: Edward Arnold, 1973).

17. The best-known attack on 'grand theory', of course, is C. W. Mills, *Sociological Imagination* (New York: Oxford University Press, 1959) ch. 2.

18. L. Althusser, *Lenin and Philosophy* (London: New Left Books, 1971) p. 72, quoted in Thompson, *The Poverty of Theory*, p. 215.

19. The phrase belongs to Geoffrey Hawthorn: see his *Enlightenment and Despair* (Cambridge University Press, 1976) p. 1.

20. Apart from Thompson, *The Poverty of Theory*, see F. Parkin, *Marxism and Class Theory: a Bourgeois Critique* (London: Tavistock, 1979), and Ley and Duncan, 'Structural Marxism and the Geography of Advanced Societies'.

21. P. Worsley, 'The Reification of Marxism: Rejoinder to Lazar', *Sociology*, 9 (3), 1975.

22. P. Abrams, 'Urban Collapse: Notes on the Non-Urban Nature of an Urban Phenomenon', in M. Harloe (ed.), *New Perspectives in Urban Change and Conflict* (London: Heinemann, 1982).

23. P. Saunders, *Urban Politics: A Sociological Interpretation* (Harmondsworth: Penguin, 1979).
24. Thompson, *The Poverty of Theory*, p. 224.
25. B. Hindess and P. Q. Hirst, *Pre-Capitalist Modes of Production* (London: Routledge & Kegan Paul, 1975) p. 312.
26. The renewed interest in urban history owes a great debt to the efforts of the late Jim Dyos, and his colleagues at Leicester University. For some impression of the scale and scope of the recent research effort in urban history, see the articles, reviews and bibliographies provided in the *Urban History Year Book* (Leicester University Press, 1974 to 1980).
27. See the collection of essays in P. Abrams and E. A. Wrigley (eds), *Towns in Societies* (Cambridge University Press, 1978), or on the Benwell CDP reports, *The Making of a Ruling Class*.
28. P. Abrams, 'Being and Becoming in Sociology' (University of Durham, 1972) p.19.
29. Foster, 'How Imperial London Preserved its Slums'.
30. Ibid, p. 111.
31. See Foster, *Class Struggles and the Industrial Revolution*, for an example of Leninist treatment of class struggle and class conflict.
32. Thompson, *The Poverty of Theory*, p. 298.
33. The phrase is Frank Parkin's: see his *Marxism and Class Theory*.
34. See N. Poulantzas, *Classes in Contemporary Capitalism* (London: New Left Books, 1975).
35. See Castells, *City, Class and Power*, pp. 170–3.
36. See A. MacLaren, *Religion and Social Class: the Disruption Years in Aberdeen* (London: Routledge & Kegan Paul, 1974).
37. F. Boal, 'Social Space in the Belfast Urban Area', pp. 225–44, and E. Jones, 'The Segregation of Roman Catholics and Protestants in Belfast', pp. 245–65, both in C. Peach, *Urban Social Segregation* (London: Longman, 1975).
38. See L. de Paor, *Divided Ulster* (Harmondsworth: Penguin, 1970).
39. M. Castells, 'Theory and Ideology in Urban Sociology', in C. Pickvance, *Urban Sociology* p. 78, or see his paper, 'Towards a Political Urban Sociology', in M. Harloe (ed.), *Captive Cities* (London: Wiley, 1977) and Harloe's own comments on Castells's approach in his introduction to the book.
40. See Castells, 'Towards a Political Urban Sociology', or David Harvey, 'Labour, Capital and Class Struggle Around the Built Environment in Advanced Capitalist Societies', in K. Cox (ed.), *Urbanization and Conflict in Market Societies* (London: Methuen, 1978), but many other instances can be found. Ley and Duncan, 'Structural Marxism and the Geography of Advanced Societies', p. 17, document this phenomenon more precisely as it appears in urban geography and, of course, the overlap between urban geography and urban sociology is considerable.
41. Thompson, *The Poverty of Theory*, p. 201.
42. The phrase is borrowed from David Ley: see his 'Social Geography and Social Action', p. 48.
43. A. Dawe, 'Theories of Social Action', in T. Bottomore and R. Nisbet

(ed), *A History of Sociological Analysis* (London: Heinemann, 1979) p. 373.

44. Ibid, p. 373.
45. Ibid, p. 375.
46. Among the CDP reports see especially those from the Benwell Studies, or the essays in Melling, *Housing, Social Policy and the State*, and our own very modest contributions B. Elliott, D. McCrone and V. Skelton, 'Property and Political Power: Edinburgh 1875–1975', pp. 92–132 in J. Garrard *et al.* (eds), *The Middle Class in Politics* (Farnborough; Saxon House, 1978), and B. Elliott and D. McCrone, 'Urban Development in Edinburgh: a Contribution to the Political Economy of Place', *Scottish Journal of Sociology*, 4, (1) 1980, pp. 1–26.
47. C. Tilly, 'The Web of Collective Action in Eighteenth Century Cities', Working paper, Centre for Research on Social Organization, University of Michigan, 1978.
48. M. Spencer, 'History and Sociology: an Analysis of Weber's *The City*', *Sociology*, 11 (3), 1977, pp. 507–25.
49. For some discussions of this see Jane Jacobs's Massey Lectures published as *Canadian Cities and Sovereignty Association* (Toronto: Canadian Broadcasting Corporation, 1980); and G. A. Nader, *Cities of Canada* (Toronto: Macmillan, 1975).
50. The classic community studies by the Lynds explored the power of a single family in Muncie, Indiana in the 1920s and 1930s: see R. S. and H. M. Lynd, *Middletown* (New York: Harcourt Brace, 1929), and their *Middletown in Transition* (New York: Harcourt Brace, 1937). In Canada, R. Lucas, *Mine Town, Mill Town, Rail Town: Life in Canadian Communities of Single Industry* (University of Toronto Press, 1971).
51. Spencer, 'History and Sociology', pp. 516–17.
52. M. Weber, *Economy and Society* (University of California Press, 1978) p. 305.
53. F. Parkin, *Marxism and Class Theory*, p. 44.

Chapter 2

1. D. Martindale, 'Prefatory Remarks', in M. Weber, *The City* (New York: Free Press, 1958) p. 56.
2. P. Abrams, 'Towns and Economic Growth: Some Theories and Some Problems', in P. Abrams and E. Wrigley, *Towns in Societies* (Cambridge University Press, 1978) p. 29.
3. T. Parsons, *The Structure of Social Action* (New York: Free Press, 1937).
4. J. Freund, *The Sociology of Max Weber* (London: Allen Lane, 1968).
5. J. Eldridge, *Max Weber: the Interpretation of Social Reality* (London: Michael Joseph, 1971).
6. A. Giddens, *Capitalism and Modern Social Theory* (Cambridge University press, 1971).
7. R. Bendix, *Max Weber: an Intellectual Portrait* (London: Methuen, 1960).
8. M. Weber, *The Protestant Ethic and the Spirit of Capitalism* (New York: Charles Schribner, 1958).
9. Bendix, *Max Weber*, p. 77.
10. Ibid, p. 72.

11. M. Weber, *Economy and Society*, ed. G. Roth and C. Wittich (University of California Press, 1978).
12. Ibid, p. 946.
13. Ibid, p. lxxxix.
14. Ibid, p. 1213.
15. Ibid, p. 1215.
16. See J. Mundy and P. Riesenberg, *The Medieval Town* (New York: Van Nostrand, 1958) p. 14.
17. Ibid, p. 37.
18. Weber, *Economy and Society*, p. 1256.
19. Ibid, p. 1259
20. H. Pirenne, *Medieval Cities* (Princeton University Press, 1948) p. 123.
21. Weber, *Economy and Society*, p. 1296.
22. Ibid, p. 1302.
23. F. Rorig, *The Medieval Town* (University of California Press, 1971).
24. Weber, *Economy and Society*, p. 1330.
25. C. Friedrichs, 'Capitalism, Mobility and Class Formation', in Abrams and Wrigley, *Towns in Societies*.
26. M. Weber, *General Economic History* (New York: Collier Books, 1966) p. 249.

Chapter 3

1. A good discussion of the role of the towns in the changing structures of rules is contained in G. Poggi, *The Development of the Modern State: a Sociological Introduction* (London; Hutchinson, 1978) ch. 3.
2. P. Clark and P. Slack, *English Towns in Transition* (Oxford University Press, 1976) p. 128.
3. For a discussion of the decline of English towns prior to the Reformation see C. Pythian-Adams, 'Urban Decay in Late Medieval England', in P. Abrams and E. A. Wrigley (eds), *Towns in Societies* (Cambridge University Press, 1978).
4. See Poggi, *The Development of the Modern State*, ch. 4.
5. P. Clark (ed.), *The Early Modern Town* (London: Longman, 1976) provides a commentary on the development of a *system* of cities, an urban hierarchy in England.
6. Poggi, *The Development of the Modern State*, p. 84.
7. If one wished to account for the character and development of towns in eastern Europe, it would be necessary to explore their location within rather different complexes of domination before, as well as after, their socialist revolutions. For some very interesting observations on this, see I. Szelenyi, 'Urban Development and Regional Management in Eastern Europe', *Theory and Society*, 10 (2), 1981, pp. 177–8.
8. C. Friedrichs, 'Capitalism, Mobility and Class Formation in the Early Modern German City', in Abrams and Wrigley, *Towns in Societies*.
9. See on this I Wallerstein, *The Modern World-System I: Capitalist Agriculture and the Origins of the European World-Economy in the 16th century* (1976); and *the Modern World-System II: Mercantilism and the Consolidation of the European*

World-Economy, 1600–1750 (New York: Academic Press, 1980).

10. I. Wallerstein, *The Modern World-System II*, ch. 6, p. 268. 'It was the emphasis in foreign trade . . . that led to Britain's emphasis on the navy and the colonies, which, in turn permitted her the military triumphs of the long struggle with France.'

11. T. M. Devine, 'Colonial Commerce and the Scottish Economy', in Cullen and Smout (eds), *Comparative Aspects of Scottish and Irish Econonmic and Social History, 1600–1900* (Edinburgh: John Donald, 1977).

12. T. C. Smout, 'Scotland and England: Is Dependency a Symptom or a Cause of Underdevelopment?', *Review III*, 4, Spring 1980, p. 618.

13. E. A. Wrigley, 'A Simple Model of London's Importance in Changing English Society and Economy 1650–1750', *Past and Present*, 37, 1967.

14. E. Hobsbawm, *Industry and Empire* (London: Weidenfield & Nicolson, 1968) p. 86.

15. See, for instance, E. Gauldie, *Cruel Habitations* (London: Allen & Unwin, 1974); A. Wohl, *The Eternal Slum: Housing and Social Policy in Victorian England* (London: Edward Arnold, 1977); H. Dyos, 'The Slums of Victorian London', *Victorian Studies*, XI, 1967.

16. D. Fraser, *Urban Politics in Victorian England* (Leicester University Press, 1976) p. 26.

17. R. Cobden, 'Incorporate your Borough! A Letter to the Inhabitants of Manchester', quoted in D. Fraser, ibid, p. 21–2.

18. S. Zukin, 'A Decade of the New Urban Sociology', *Theory and Society*, 9 (4), 1980, p. 590.

19. H. Meller, *Leisure and the Changing City, 1870–1914* (London: Routledge & Kegan Paul, 1976).

20. A. D. Gilbert, *Religion and Society in Industrial England* (London: Longman, 1976).

21. S. E. Barker, 'Orange and Green: Belfast, 1832–1912', in H. Dyos and M. Wolff (eds), *The Victorian City; Images and Realities*, vol. 2 (London: Routledge & Kegan Paul, 1973).

22. E. P. Hennock, *Fit and Proper Persons: Ideal and Reality in 19th Century Urban Government* (London: Edward Arnold, 1973) p. 185.

23. Ibid, p. 185.

24. J. Garrard, 'Leaders and Politics in Nineteenth-century Salford: an Historical Analysis of Political Power', Salford City Politics Research Series, University of Salford, Dept of Sociology and Political Studies, 1977.

25. A study of Glasgow's middle-class housing areas illustrates this point. see M. A. Simpson and T. H. Lloyd, *Middle Class Housing in Britain* (Newton Abbot: David & Charles, 1977).

26. Our study of Edinburgh councillors shows clearly that 'property interests' were very heavily involved in those committees of the council which dealt with matters of planning and development. See B. Elliott, D. McCrone and V. Skelton, 'Property and Politics: Edinburgh 1875–1975', in *The Middle Class in Politics*, J. Garrard *et al.* (eds) (Farnborough: Saxon House, 1978).

27. R. Williams, *The Country and the City* (Oxford University Press, 1973) p. 220.
28. P. Joyce, *Work, Society and Politics; the culture of the factory in Later Victorian England* (Sussex: Harvester Press, 1980) p. 292.
29. The most extensive discussion of this is found in M. Foucault, *Discipline and Punish; the Birth of the Prison* (Harmondsworth: Penguin, 1977).
30. 'Should I subscribe to the Industrial School? or reasons for the education of pauper children' (Aberdeen 1850), quoted in A. A. MacLaren, *Religion and Social Class* (London: Routledge & Kegan Paul, 1974) p. 157.
31. Ibid, p. 150.
32. Joyce, *Work, Society and Politics*, p. 278.
33. A. Briggs, *Victorian Cities* (Harmondsworth: Penguin, 1968) p. 165.
34. Hennock, *Fit and Proper Persons*.
35. Ibid, pp. 314–15.
36. Report of the Royal Sanitary Commission (Adderley Commission) 1871, p.16; quoted in G. Best, *Mid-Victorian Britain, 1851–75* (London: Weidenfeld & Nicolson, 1971) p. 40.
37. *Progressive Association*, Local Government Manifesto, 1973 (Edinburgh Public Library).
38. For the best discussions of the ideal of non-partisanship, see K. Young, 'The Politics of London Government 1880–99', *Public Administration*, 51, 1973; and W. P. Grant, 'Non-Partisanship in Britain Local Politics', *Policy and Politics*, 1, 1972–3.
39. R. S. Neale, *Class and Ideology in the Nineteenth Century* (London: Routledge & Kegan Paul, 1972).
40. G. Crossick, *An Artisan Elite in Victorian London: Kentish London, 1840–1880* (London: Croom Helm, 1978) ch. 10.
41. E. P. Hennock, *Fit and Proper Persons*, p. 327.
42. For a fascinating account of the different trajectories of labour struggle, see J. M. Smith, 'Commonsense Thought and Working-Class Consciousness: Some Aspects of Glasgow and Liverpool Labour Movements in the Early Years of the 20th century', Ph.D., Edinburgh, 1981; and for further details on Liverpool, P. J. Waller, *Democracy and Sectarianism: a Political and Social History of Liverpool, 1868–1939* (Liverpool University Press, 1981).
43. Wohl, *The Eternal Slum*, pp. 73–4.
44. S. G. Checkland, *The Upas Tree: Glasgow, 1875–1975, a Study in Growth and Contraction* (Glasgow University Press, 1976) p. 92.
45. P. Abrams, 'Towns and Economic Growth: Some Theories and Problems', in Abrams and Wrigley (eds), *Towns in Societies*, p. 39.

Chapter 4

1. P. Dunleavy, *Urban Political Analysis* (London: Macmillan, 1980) p.60.
2. Ibid, pp. 58 and 59.

3. *Social Trends*, 11, 1981, table 5.8, 'People in employment: by sector',
    pp. 74–76.
4. M. Weber, *Economy and Society* (University of California Press, 1968)
    p. 991.
5. M. Weber, 'Politics as a Vocation', in W. G. Runciman (ed.), *Weber:
    Selections in Translation* (Cambridge University Press, 1978); For
    discussion of Weber's views on politics and bureaucracy, see D.
    Beetham, *Max Weber and the Theory of Modern Politics* (London: Allen &
    Unwin, 1972) ch. 10; and A. Giddens, *Politics and Sociology in the Thought of
    Max Weber* (London: Macmillan, 1972).
6. Tom Burns, 'Sovereignty, Interests and Bureaucracy in the Modern
    State', *British Journal of Sociology*, 31 (4), 1980, p. 498.
7. R. Pahl, 'Urban Managerialism Re-considered', *Whose City?*
    (Harmondsworth: Penguin, 1975, 2nd edn) ch. 13.
8. M. Lipsky, 'Towards a Theory of Street-level Bureaucracy', in W. D.
    Hawley and M. Lipsky, *Theoretical Perspectives on Urban Politics* (New
    Jersey: Prentice-Hall, 1976); J. M. Prottas, *People Processing; the Street-
    level Bureaucrat in Public Service Bureaucracies* (Toronto: Lexington Books,
    1979).
9. Prottas, *People Processing*, p. 87.
10. Dunleavy, *Urban Political Analysis*, p. 54.
11. J. Dearlove, *the Reorganisation of British Local Government: Old Orthodoxies
    and a Political Perspective* (Cambridge University Press, 1979) p. 221.
12. P. Saunders, *Urban Politics: a Sociological Interpretation* (Harmondsworth:
    Penguin, 1979) p. 196.
13. C. Cockburn, *The Local State* (London: Pluto Press, 1977) p. 45.
14. Ibid, p. 42.
15. M. Hill, *The Sociology of Public Administration* (London: Weidenfeld &
    Nicolson, 1972) p. 199.
16. K. Newton, 'Turnout and Marginality in Local Elections', *British Journal
    of Political Science*, 2, 1972; and K. Newton, *Second City Politics* (Oxford
    University Press, 1976).
17. Dunleavy, *Urban Political Analysis*, pp. 112–19; Hill, *The Sociology of Public
    Administration*, ch. 10; T. J. Johnson, *Professions and Power* (London:
    Macmillan, 1972); N. Dennis, *People and Planning* (London: Faber,
    1970).
18. W. H. Cox, *Cities: the Public Dimension* (Harmondsworth: Penguin, 1976)
    p. 138.
19. H. H. Heclo, 'The Councillor's Job', *Public Administration*, 47, 1969,
    p. 188.
20. Hill, *The Sociology of Public Administration*, ch. 11.
21. R. J. Buxton, *Local Government* (Harmondsworth: Penguin, 1970)
    pp. 269–70.
22. J. M. Lee, *Social Leaders and Public Persons* (Oxford University Press,
    1963) pp. 212–14.
23. L. J. Sharpe, 'Theories and Values in Local Government', *Political
    Studies*, 18 (2), 1970.
24. Cox, *Cities*, p. 55.

25. Dennis, *People and Planning;* Saunders, *Urban Politics,* ch. 3; P. Leonard, 'The Sociology of Community Action', *Sociological Review Monograph,* 21, 1975; N. Wates, *The Battle for Tolmers Square* (London: Routledge & Kegan Paul, 1976).

26. Dennis, *People and Planning;* N. Dennis, *Public Participation and Planners' Blight* (London: Faber, 1972).

27. Jon Gower Davies, *The Evangelistic Bureaucrat* (London: Tavistock, 1972).

28. S. Damer and C. Hague, 'Public Participation in Planning: a Review'; *Town Planning Review,* 42 (3), 1971; J. Dearlove, *The Politics of Policy in Local Government: the Making and Maintenance of Public Policy in Kensington and Chelsea* (Cambridge University Press, 1973).

29. K. Young, *Local Politics and the Rise of Party: the London Municipal Society and the Conservative Intervention in Local Elections, 1894–1963* (Leicester University Press, 1975).

30. B. Elliott, D. McCrone and V. Skelton, 'Property and Political Power: Edinburgh, 1875–1975', in J. Garrard *et al., The Middle Class in Politics* (Farnborough: Saxon House, 1978).

31. Dearlove, *The Reorganisation of British Local Government,* p. 145.

32. Hill, *The Sociology of Public Administration,* p. 211.

33. K. Newton, 'City Politics in Britain and the United States', *Political Studies,* 17, 1969.

34. Cox, *Cities,* p. 123.

35. Dunleavy, *Urban Political Analysis,* p. 62, table 3.4.

36. Dearlove, *The Politics of Policy in Local Government,* p. 20.

37. For its changing implications for local–central relations, see P. Saunders, 'Local Government and the State', *New Society,* 13 March 1980.

38. 'Tory Bill "Socialist Trojan Horse"', *The Guardian,* 5 February 1980.

39. K. Young and J. Kramer, *Strategy and Conflict in Metropolitan Housing: Suburbia versus the Greater London Council, 1965–1975* (London: Heinemann, 1978).

40. Sharpe, 'Theories and Values in Local Government', p. 153.

41. C. Reich, 'The New Property', *Yale Law Journal,* 73, 1964; also Elliott, McCrone and Skelton, 'Property and Political Power', p. 128.

42. Peta Sheriff has provided a valuable bibliography entitled, 'The Sociology of Public Bureaucracy, 1965–1975', in *Current Sociology,* 24 (2), 1976.

43. M. Spencer, 'History and Sociology: an Analysis of Weber's *The City*', *Sociology,* 11 (3), 1977.

44. S. Damer, 'Wine Alley: the Sociology of a Dreadful Enclosure', *Sociological Review,* 22, 1974.

45. For an analysis of that quintessential bureaucratic control mechanism, the queue, see J. Lambert, C. Paris and B. Blackaby, *Housing Policy and the State: Allocation, Access and Control* (London: Macmillan, 1978) ch. 3.

46. Lipsky, 'Towards a Theory of Street-level Bureaucracy'.

47. Prottas, *People Processing,* p. 7.

Chapter 5

1. Some of the most acute observations on the institution of private property are found in the work of C. B. Macpherson. See his article 'Capitalism and the Changing Concept of Property', pp. 104–25, in E. Kamenka and R. S. Neale, *Feudalism, Capitalism and Beyond* (London: Edward Arnold, 1975).
2. M. Weber, *Economy and Society* (University of California Press, 1978) p. 928.
3. See, for instance, H. Richardson, J. Vipond and R. Furbey, *Housing and Urban Spatial Structure* (Farnborough: Saxon House, 1975); or C. Peach (ed.), *Urban Social Segregation* (London: Longman, 1975).
4. J. Parry Lewis, *Building Cycles and Britain's Economic Growth* (London: Macmillan, 1965).
5. Of the 200 landlords we interviewed as part of our project, 54 per cent had inherited some or all of the properties they owned.
6. This is the theme Thernstrom explores when looking at the pattern of owner-occupation among migrants to the USA in the nineteenth century. S. Thernstrom, *Poverty and Progress: Social Mobility in a Nineteenth-Century City* (Cambridge, Mass.: Harvard University Press, 1974).
7. T. H. Marshall, *Sociology at the Crossroads* (London: Heinemann, 1963) p. 239.
8. We have discussed the traditional powers of landlords in a forthcoming article, 'The Social World of Petty Property', in P. Hollowell (ed.), *Property and Social Relations* (London: Heinemann, 1982) and in an earlier conference paper, 'Property Relations in the City: the Fortunes of Landlordism', in M. Harloe (ed.), *Proceedings of the Conference on Urban Change and Conflict* (London: Centre for Environmental Studies, 1975).
9. Elliott and McCrone, 'The Social World of Petty Property'.
10. See J. Rose, in *Investors Chronicle*, 21 December 1979.
11. J. Lorimer *The Developers* (Toronto: James Lorimer, 1978).
12. L. Gertler and R. Crowley, *Changing Canadian Cities: the Next 25 Years* (Toronto: McClelland & Stewart, 1977), show that Canada's rate of urban growth has outstripped that of any other western nation since 1945.
13. O. Marriott, *The Property Boom* (London: Pan Books, 1967).
14. Marriot, *ibid;* S. Jenkins, *Landlords to London: Story of a Capital and its Growth* (London: Constable, 1975); Counter Information Services, *The Recurrent Crisis of London: Anti-report on the Property Developers* (London: Constable/CIS, 1973).
15. Marriott, *The Property Boom*, p. 21.
16. There is a very real need for research on land-assembly operations, as indeed there is for general studies of the construction and development industry in Britain.
17. Lorimer, *The Developers, passim.*
18. *The Guardian*, 16 June 1972.
19. Gerson Berger, *Investors Chronicle*, 6 May 1977, p. 499.
20. See the report by the Benwell CDP, *Benwell's Hidden Property Companies*

(Newcastle, 1976).

21. See the Milner Holland findings, *Report of the Committee on Housing in Greater London*, Cmnd 2604 (London: HMSO, 1965).

22. The Holloway Neighbourhood Law Centre report, 'David and Goliath' (Barnsbury, 1973) (no page number).

23. See Marriott, *The Property Boom*, p. 177.

24. Geoffrey Wilson, 'Government Recognises the Role of the Developer', *Investors Chronicle*, 9 November 1979, p. 13.

25. Some discussion of Edinburgh's property companies is contained in our paper, 'Landlords in Edinburgh: Some Preliminary Findings', *Sociological Review*, 23 (3), 1975. The same point was made in Benwell CDP's *Benwell's Hidden Property Companies*, p. 17.

26. .J. Rose, *Investors Chronicle*, 21 December 1979.

27. R. Minns, *Pension Funds and British Capitalism* (London: Heinemann, 1980).

28. A useful analysis of changing tenure patterns in England and Wales is provided in Central Statistical Office, *Social Trends* (London: HMSO, 1979).

29. In the American literature, the most explicit formulation of the hypotheses, and the best debunking of most of them, is contained in B. Berger, *Working Class Suburb* (Berkeley: University of California Press, 1960). For appraisal of the British versions of the arguments, see J. H. Goldthorpe *et al.*, *The Affluent Worker: Political Attitudes and Behaviour* (Cambridge University Press, 1968).

30. One of the earliest studies was R. Durant, *Watling: a Survey of Social Life on a New Housing Estate* (London: P. S. King, 1939), and in the 1950s and 1960s other accounts of local communities complemented her discussion. See T. Lupton and D. Mitchell, *Neighbourhood and Community* (Liverpool University Press, 1954); P. Collison, *The Cutteslowe Walls* (London: Faber & Faber, 1963); M. Stacey, *Tradition and Change* (Oxford University Press, 1960); N. Elias and J. Scotson, *The Established and the Outsiders* (London: Cass, 1962).

31. See, for instance, K. Young and J. Kramer, 'Local Exclusionary Policies in Britain: the Case of Suburban Defence in a Metropolitan System', in K. Cox, *Urbanization and Conflict in Market Societies* (London: Methuen, 1978), or P. Saunders, *Urban Politics: a Sociological Interpretation* (Harmondsworth: Penguin, 1978).

32. J. Rex and R. Moore, *Race, Community and Conflict: a Study of Sparkbrook* (Oxford University Press, 1967).

33. J. Rex, 'The Sociology of the Zone of Transition', in R. Pahl (ed.), *Readings in Urban Sociology* (Oxford: Pergamon, 1968).

34. R. Haddon, 'The Location of West Indians in the London Housing Market', *New Atlantis*, 2 (1), 1970.

35. P. Saunders, 'Domestic Property and Social Class', *International Journal of Urban and Regional Research*, 2 (2), 1978, p. 238. The argument also appears as chapter 2 in his book *Urban Politics: a Sociological Interpretation* (Harmondsworth: Penguin, 1979).

36. R. Barrell and M. Farmer, 'Homes or Jobs: Maggie's choice', *The*

Observer, 21 October 1979. This same theme has also been discussed in the broader economic arguments of H. Leyer and G. Edwards, in two articles in the *Sunday Times*, 2 November and 9 November 1980, where they claim that the very favourable rates of return on home ownership, and property more generally, have done much to limit the flows of capital to Britain's ailing productive industries.

37. Central Statistical Office, *Social Trends* (London: HMSO, 1974).
38. See the *Investors Chronicle*, 7 November 1980.

Chapter 6

1. M. Castells, *City, Class and Power* (London: Macmillan, 1978) p. 167.
2. D. Bell, *The Coming of Post-Industrial Society* (New York: Basic Books, 1973); A. Touraine, *The Post-Industrial Society* (New York: Random House, 1971).
3. On the expansion of white-collar work and the growth of unionism in this section of the workforce, see R. F. Elliott, 'The Growth of White Collar Employment in Great Britain 1951–1971', *British Journal of Industrial Relations*, XV (i), March 1977, and R. Price and G. Bain, 'Union Growth Revisited: 1948–74 in Perspective', *British Journal of Industrial Relations*, XIV (3), 1976.
4. The best-known examination of these differences is D. Lockwood, *The Black-coated Worker* (London: Allen & Unwin, 1966).
5. The point is made in many sources. See. J. Westergaard and H. Resler, *Class in a Capitalist Society* (London: Heinemann, 1975); A. B. Atkinson (ed.), *Wealth, Income and Inequality* (Harmondsworth, Penguin, 1973); A. B. Atkinson, *Unequal Shares: Wealth In Britain* (London: Allen Lane, 1972); or *An A to Z of Income and Wealth,* the last publication of the Royal Commission on Income and Wealth (London: HMSO, 1980).
6. A recent study commenting on this phenomenon is that by O. Gill, *Luke Street* (London: Macmillan, 1979).
7. J. Rex, 'Black Militancy and Class Conflict', in R. Miles and A. Phizacklea, *Racism and Political Action in Britain* (London: Routledge & Kegan Paul, 1979).
8. See the journal, *Race Today*, or the book by R. Moore, *Racism and Black Resistance* (London: Pluto Press, 1975), which draws heavily on this and other black press sources.
9. With our colleague, Frank Bechhofer, we have written about this. See F. Bechhofer, B. Elliott and D. McCrone, 'Structure, Consciousness and Action: a Sociological Profile of the British Middle Class', *British Journal of Sociology*, XXIX (4), 1978. See too, K. Roberts, F. Cook, S. Clark and E. Semeonoff, *The Fragmentary Class Structure* (London: Heinemann, 1977).
10. C. Hartman, *Yerba Buena: Land Grab and Community Resistance in San Francisco* (National Housing and Economic Development Law Project, Earl Warren Legal Institution, Berkeley: University of California Press, 1974) p. 106.

11. D. Ley, 'Liberal Ideology and the Post-Industrial City', *Annals of the Association of American Geographers*, 70 (2), 1980.
12. Ibid, p. 258.
13. The best-known works commenting on the changing character of the Labour Party are: B. Hindess, *The Decline of Working Class Politics* (London: Paladin, 1971), and T. Forester, *The Labour Party and the Working Class* (London: Heinemann, 1976).
14. For details of changes in party composition at a national level, see R. W. Johnson, 'The British Political Elite, 1955–1972', *Archives Européen de Sociologie*, XIV, 1973.
15. An amusing portrait of a traditional, long-dominant local party is contained in M. Bulmer, 'Tammany Hall beside the Wear', *New Society*, 24 November 1977.
16. See Moore, *Racism and Black Resistance,* for a description of the disputes at the Mansfield Hosiery works or the Imperial Typewriter company, perhaps the best-known instances where black workers were not supported by the predominantly white unions.
17. A collection of articles dealing with the so-called middle-class revolt is found in R. King and N. Nugent, *Reluctant Rebels* (London: Hodder & Stoughton, 1979).
18. For evidence of this, see the recent report by Members of Parliament, in *The Joint Committee against Racialism,* and newspaper commentary on this. For instance, *The Sunday Times*, 8 February 1981.
19. Their formation is documented in many issues of *Race Today*. For a plea to co-ordinate self-defence for Asians and West Indians see the article by Darcus Howe, *Race Today*, October 1978. For a recent example of an organisation concerned with the defence of a local black community, see newspaper coverage of the New Cross Massacre Action Committee.
20. J. Kirkpatrick 'Politics and the New Class', *Transaction*, 16 (2), 1979.
21. Bell, *The Coming of Post-Industrial Society.*
22. R. Miliband, 'A State of De-Subordination', *British Journal of Sociology*, XXIX (4), 1978.
23. See the recent books by P. Saunders, *Urban Politics: a Sociological Interpretation* (Harmondsworth: Penguin, 1980), and P. Dunleavy, *Urban Political Analysis* (London: Macmillan, 1980).
24. C. Cockburn, *The Local State* (London: Pluto Press, 1977).
25. P. Saunders, 'Towards a Non-spatial Urban Sociology', Working Paper 31, Urban and Regional Studies, University of Sussex, July, 1980 and elements of the argument are to be found in his book *Social Theory and the Urban Question* (London: Hutchinson, 1981).
26. M. Castells, 'Is There an Urban Sociology?', in C. Pickvance (ed.), *Urban Sociology: Critical Essays* (London: Tavistock, 1976).
27. P. Dunleavy, 'The Urban Basis of Political Alignment', *British Journal of Political Science*, 9 (4) 1979.
28. M. Castells, 'Urban Social Movements and the Struggle for Democracy: the Citizens' Movement in Spain', *International Journal of Urban and Regional Research*, 2 (1), March 1978; J. Olives, 'The Struggle Against Urban Renewal in the Cité d'Aliarte' (Paris), in Pickvance, *Urban*

Sociology.

29. Touraine, *The Post-Industrial Society.*
30. Among a great many studies see: C. Bell and H. Newby, 'Community Communion, Class and Community Action', in D. Herbert and R. R. Johnson (eds), *Social Geography and the Study of Urban Areas* (London: Wiley, 1977); D. Donnison, 'The Micro-Politics of the City', in D. Donnison and D. Eversley (eds), *London: Urban Patterns, Problems and Policies* (London: Heinemann, 1973); P. Leonard (ed.), 'The Sociology of Community Action', *Sociological Review Monograph,* no. 21, 1975; J. O'Malley, *The Politics of Community Action* (Nottingham: Spokesman Books, 1977); D. Perman, *Cublington: Blueprint for Resistance* (Oxford: Bodley Head, 1972); N. Wates, *The Battle for Tolmers Square* (London: Routledge & Kegan Paul, 1976).
32. M. Harrington, 'The New Class and the Left', *Transaction,* 16 (2), 1979.
33. A Marsh, *Protest and Political Consciousness* (Beverly Hills: Sage, 1977).

Chapter 7

1. I. Szelenyi, 'Structural Changes of and Alternatives to Capitalist Development in the Contemporary Urban and Regional System', *International Journal of Urban and Regional Research,* 5 (1), 1981, pp. 1–14.
2. The problem was by no means confined to *urban* sociology. Elsewhere in the subject a similar enthusiasm for 'theory' and disdain for all but very simple methods of empirical work could be observed. For some comment on general trends in methodology, see F. Bechhofer, 'Substantive Dogs and Methodological Tails: A Question of Fit', *Sociology,* 15 (4), 1981.
3. P. Townsend, 'By restricting the flow of information, the Government is restricting the right to free and open discussion of the industrial, economic and social conditions of Britain', *The Guardian,* 15 July 1981.
4. R. Friedland, F. F. Piven and R. Alford, 'Political Conflict, Urban Structure and the Fiscal Crisis', *International Journal of Urban and Regional Research,* 1 (3), 1977, p. 450.
5. E. P. Thompson, *Writing by Candlelight* (London: Merlin, 1980).
6. See, for instance, F. Fox Piven and R. Cloward, *Poor People's Movements* (New York: Pantheon Books, 1977).
7. The best discussion of repertoires of protest is found in C. Tilly, *From Mobilization to Revolution* (Reading, Massachusetts: Addison-Wesley, 1978).
8. See especially B. Roberts, *Cities of Peasants* (London: Edward Arnold, 1978), or W. Cornelius and F. Trueblood (eds), *Latin American Urban Research,* 4 and 5 (Beverly Hills: Sage, 1974 and 1975).
9. For example, P. Lloyd, *Slums of Hope* (Harmondsworth: Penguin, 1979): and, though they go well beyond a concern with strictly urban phenomena, the readings in P. Gutkind and I. Wallerstein (eds), *The Political Economy of Contemporary Africa* (Beverly Hills: Sage, 1976); P. Gutkind and P. Waterman (eds), *African Social Studies: a Radical Reader* (London: Heinemann, 1975); E. de Kadt and G. Williams, *Sociology and*

Development (London: Tavistock, 1974).

10. See I. Szelenyi, 'Urban Development and Regional Management in Eastern Europe', *Theory and Society*, 10 (2), 1981, pp. 169–205.

11. For some description of urbanization in Canada, see L. Gertler and R. Crowley, *Changing Canadian Cities: the Next 25 Years* (Toronto: McClelland & Stewart, 1979); J. W. Simmons, *The Canadian Urban System* (University of Toronto Press, 1977); N. Lithwick, *Urban Canada: Problems and Prospects* (Ottawa: Central Mortgage and Housing Corporation, 1970). For some recent work on Australian cities, see L. Sandercock, *Cities for Sale* (University of Melbourne Press, 1976); L. Kilmartin and D. Thorns, *Cities Unlimited* (Sydney: Allen & Unwin, 1978); H. Stretton, *Ideas for Australian Cities* (Adelaide: the Author, 1970).

12. D. Donnison and P. Soto, *The Good City* (London: Heinemann, 1980).

13. Ibid, p. 46.

14. R. Krohn, and his colleagues in Montreal, carried out a study of the 'alternative' economy in the housing market and showed how, in immigrant communities, people bought and refurbished homes by sharing labour and resources: R. Krohn, B. Fleming and M. Manzer, *The Other Economy: the Internal Logic of Local Rental Housing* (Toronto: Peter Martin Associates, 1977). Rex and Moore showed how immigrant landlords raised money from sources other than the banks and building societies in order to gain a toe-hold in the housing market: see J. Rex and R. Moore, *Race, Community and Conflict* (Oxford University Press, 1967).

15. This last is used in 'Urban Development and Regional Management in Eastern Europe', by Szelenyi, following Lefebvre. See Szelenyi, and his article, 'The Relative Autonomy of the State or the State Mode of Production', in M. J. Dear and A. J. Scott (eds), *Urbanization and Urban Planning in Capitalist Societies* (London: Methuen, 1980).

16. See, for instance, J. Smith, 'The Informal Economy', *Lloyds Bank Review*, 141, 1981.

17. J. Gershuny and R. Pahl, 'Work Outside Employment: Some Preliminary Speculation', *New Universities Quarterly*, 34, 1979–80, pp. 120–35; J. Gershuny, 'The Informal Economy', *Futures*, February 1979; J. Gershuny and R. Pahl, 'Britain in the Decade of Three Economies', *New Society*, 3 January 1980.

18. Roberts, *Cities of Peasants*.

19. Along with some of our colleagues at Edinburgh we have written about some of this. See B. Elliott, F. Bechhofer, D. McCrone and S. Black, 'Bourgeois Social Movements in Britain: Repertoires and Responses', forthcoming in *Sociological Review*. Other papers reporting the results of our study will appear subsequently.

20. Thompson, *Writing by Candlelight*.

Index

Aberdeen 18
Abrams, P. 13, 15, 33, 49n, 53n, 77n
Alford, R. 141
Althusser, L. 3, 7, 12–16, 19
Atkinson, A. B. 120n
Australia 143
authority 27–8

Bain, G. 119n
Baker, S. E. 65n
Barrell, R. 114n
Bechhofer, F. 120n, 139n, 147n
Beetham, D. 80n
Belfast 18, 65
Bell, C. 136n
Bell, D. 119, 127
Bendix, R. 35, 36
Benwell, C. D. P. 105, 108n
Berger, B. 111n
Berger, G. 105n
Best, G. 70n
Birmingham 63–4, 73, 144
Black, S. 147n
Blackaby, B. 94n
Boal, F. 18n
Bottomore, T. 20n
bourgeoisie 45, 59, 63–71
  industrial bourgeoisie 61–6
  petite-bourgeoisie 31, 57, 69–73,
    98–101, 120, 125, 147
Bradford 68
Braudel, F. 8n
Briggs, A. 68
Bristol 59, 64–5
Bulmer, M. 125n
bureaucracy 75, 77, 78–96
  power of 133–7, 149
  street-level bureaucracy 81, 95
burghers 41, 45, 46–50, 56–61
Burns, T. 4, 80
Buxton, R. J. 85

Canada 17, 24, 30, 102, 143
capitalism, growth of 49, 50, 56–72
Castells, M. 6, 7, 9, 10, 13, 15, 16,
  19, 88, 118, 130, 132
charisma 27
Checkland, S. 75
Chicago School 8
civic pride 68
Clark, P. 52, 54n
class 9, 29–31
  class consciousness 15–16
  class struggle 8, 9, 17, 31–2, 37,
    122, 138
  intra-class conflict 17, 71, 76
  politics of class 130–3
Cloward, R. 142n
Cobden, R. 63
Cockburn, C. 9, 83, 129n
collective consumption 9, 10, 92
Collison, P. 111n
Community Development Project 22
conjurations, oath-bound association
  40, 44, 46–7
Conservative Party 86, 88, 128, 147
  Conservative Government 91, 147
  Tory, Toryism 67, 72, 124, 149
consumer city 39
Cornelius, W. 143n
corporate cities 51, 143
corporation, city corporation 47–8, 55,
  85
  incorporation 63–6
Counter Information Services 102
Cox, K. 19n, 112n
Cox, W. H. 84n, 87, 90n
Crossick, G. 73n
Crowley, R. 102n, 143n

Damer, S. 88n, 94n
Davies, J. D. 88
Dawe, A. 20–1

Dear, M. J.   145n
Dearlove, J.   82, 88n, 89, 91
democracy   105–6
   democratic control   94, 140–2, 149
Dennis, N.   84n, 88, 133n
Devine, T. M.   59n
domination   27–8, 32, 36, 43
   bourgeois domination   66–72
   bureaucratic domination   79, 83–7
   cultural domination   134–5
   non-legitimate domination   37, 41
Donnison, D.   136n, 144
Duncan, J.   7n, 13n, 19n
Dundee   129, 151
Dunleavy, P.   78, 82, 84n, 90, 128, 132
Durant, R.   111n
Dyos, H.   14n, 62n, 65n

Eastern Europe   138, 143
economy, economy parties   69–70
Edinburgh   24, 31, 72–3, 88, 103
Eldridge, J.   35
Elias, N.   111n
Elliott, B.   22n, 66n, 88n, 101n,
   108n, 120n, 147n
Elliott, R. F.   119n
England   46, 47, 52, 54, 57, 59, 60
ethnicity   17–18, 23, 32
   race   112, 120, 126–8, 141
   racial harassment   149
Eversley, D.   136n

Farmer, M.   114
feudalism   34, 38–40, 47–8
Forester, T.   124n
formal and informal economy 145–6
Foster, J.   8n, 9n, 15
Foucault, M.   67n
Fraser, D.   62n
Freund, J.   35
Friedland, R.   141
Friedrichs, C.   8n, 49, 56, 57
functionalism   12
Furbey, R.   98n

Garrard, J.   66, 66n, 88n
Gauldie, E.   62n
gentrification   105, 115
German cities   39, 41–2, 46
Gershuny, J.   146
Gertler, L.   120n, 143n
Giddens, A.   21, 35, 80n
Gilbert, A. D.   64–5

Gill, O.   120n
Glasgow   18, 24, 59, 61, 73, 75, 144
Goldthorpe, J. H.   111n
Grant, W.   72n
guilds   52–3, 56–7
Gutkind, P.   143n

Haddon, R.   112
Hague, C.   88n
Harloe, M.   6n, 13n, 19n, 101n
Harrington, M.   136
Hartman, C.   122n
Harvey, D.   11, 19n
Hawley, W. D.   81n
Hawthorn, G.   13n
Heclo, H. H.   84
Hennock, E. P.   66, 69, 73
Herbert, D.   136n
Hill, M.   83, 84n, 85, 89
Hindess, B.   14, 124n
Hirst, P. Q.   14
Hobsbawm, E.   4, 61
Hollowell, P.   101n
housing   74–8, 91, 94–5
   housing classes   112
   owner-occupation   111–15, 126
   public housing   9, 148

Italian cities   38, 41, 43, 45–8

Jacobs, J.   24n
Jenkins, S.   102
Johnson, R.   136n
Johnson, R. W.   124n
Johnson, T. J.   84n
Joyce, P.   67n, 68n

Kadt, E. de   143n
Kamenka, E.   97n
King, R.   126n
Kirkpatrick, J.   127
Kramer, J.   91, 112
Krohn, R.   145n

Labour Party   73–6, 84–5, 120, 123–5
   Labour Government   115
Lambert, J.   94n
landlords   99–101, 116
Lee, J. M.   86
Leeds   62, 66, 68, 73
Lefebvre, H.   6
legitimacy   66–72

legitimation 27–8
Leonard, P. 10n, 87n
Lewis, J. Parry 100n
Ley, D. 7, 13n, 19n, 122
Liberal Party 73, 124
Lipsky, M. 81, 95
Lithwick, N. 143n
Liverpool 18, 59, 61, 74
Lloyd, P. 143n
Lloyd, T. H. 66n
local state 83, 90–1, 129
localism 70–1
Lockwood, D. 21, 119n
Lojkine, J. 6, 9n
London 54, 60–1, 88
Londonderry 18
Lorimer, J. 102, 104, 107
Lucas, R. 27n
Lupton, T. 111n
Lynd, R. S. 27n

McCrone, D. 22n, 66n, 88n, 101n,
    108n, 120n, 147n
MacLaren, A. 18n, 67n
Macpherson, C. B. 97n
Manchester 62, 63, 64, 84
Marriott, O. 102, 103, 107n
Marsh, A. 137n
Marshall, T. H. 100
Martindale, D. 33, 44
Marx, Karl 3, 8, 12, 19, 21, 23
Marxism in urban sociology 2–4, 6–32
    criticisms of 11–20, 138–9
    structural Marxism 3, 7, 11–20, 138
Meller, H. 64n
Melling, J. 8n, 22n
merchants 40, 57–61
middle class 87, 133
    bureaucratic, technocratic middle
        class 93, 96, 120–6
    service class 127–8
Miles, R. 120n
Miliband, R. 9n, 127
Miller, S. M. 10
Mills, C. Wright 12n
Minns, R. 110
Mitchell, D. 111n
monarchy 41, 47–8, 52–8
Moore, R. 112, 120n, 126n, 145n
Mundy, J. 40

Nader, G. A. 24n

nation-state 25, 42, 51–6, 90
    the state and urban development
        116–17
Neale, R. S. 73, 97n
neo-fascist organizations 1, 127
neo-fascist ideas 153
new right 147–50, 152
new urban sociology 2, 4, 6, 8, 138
Newby, H. 136n
Newton, K. 84n, 90n
Nisbet, R. 20n
non-partisanship 70, 71
Nugent, N. 126n

Olives, J. 10, 132n
O'Malley, J. 136n

Pahl, R. 9n, 10, 80, 92, 146
Paor, L. de 18n
Paris 54, 118
Paris, C. 94n
Parkin, F. 13n, 16n, 30, 31
Parsons, T. 35
party 26, 43, 126
patrician city 34, 42–5
    patricians 42–3, 49
Peach, C. 18n, 98n
pension funds 109–10, 117
Perman, D. 136n
Phizacklea, A. 120n
Pickvance, C. 6n, 19n
Pirenne, H. 43
Piven, F. F. 141, 142n
plebeian city 34, 45–6
    plebeians 48
    popolo 37, 45–6
podestà 43–5
Poggi, G. 51n, 53n, 55
policing 1, 5, 142–3, 149
post-industrial city 122
    post-industrial society 119, 133
Poulantzas, N. 9n, 16
power 28, 34–6
producer city 34, 39
property developers 101–11, 117, 122,
    131
property relations 97–101, 147
Price, R. 119n
Prottas, J. M. 81, 95
public property 92, 95, 129
    and the service stratum 120–1, 134
Pythian-Adams, C. 53n

ratepayers 70
  ratepayers' groups 90, 126
Reich, C. 92n
Resler, H. 120n
religion, religious differentiation 18, 23, 30, 64–6, 77
  Anglicans 77
  Catholics 18, 30
  Dissenters 64–5, 73, 77
  Protestant ethic 35–6, 146
  and social control 68
rentiers 36, 41, 45, 131
Rex, J. 112, 120, 145n
Richardson, H. 98n
Riesenberg, P. 40
Roberts, B. 143, 146
Roberts, K. 120n
Rorig, F. 48
Rose, J. 101n, 108
Roth, G. 36
Runciman, W. G. 80n

Samuels, M. 7n
Sandercock, L. 143n
Saunders, P. 13, 82, 87n, 91n, 112n, 113, 128n, 129, 130
Scotland 60, 64, 68, 134, 143, 148, 150
Scotson, J. 111n
Scott, A. J. 145n
shanty towns 8
Sharpe, L. J. 87, 91n
Shelter 126
Sheriff, P. 93n
Simmons, J. W. 143n
Simpson, M. A. 66n
Skelton, V. 22n 66n, 88n
Slack, P. 52
Smith, J. 146n
Smith, J. M. 74n
Smout, T. C. 59n
social consumption, social investment 130
social closure 30, 31
Soto, P. 144
Spencer, M. 23–4, 28, 93
Stacey, M. 111n
Standestaat 51–3
status, status groups 18, 29, 35–6, 76, 120
Stretton, H. 143n
Szelenyi, I. 56n, 138, 143, 145n, 152

Thernstrom, S. 100n
Thompson, E. P. 4, 9n, 12, 14, 16, 19, 141, 151
Thorns, D. 143n
Tilly, C. 4, 23n, 142n
Touraine, A. 119, 133
Townsend, P. 140
Trueblood, F. 143n

United States of America 90, 118, 144, 147
urban autonomy 35, 40–2, 90–1
  rise and decline of 46–50
urban decay 58, 102
urban geography 7, 19n
urban managers 80–1, 92–3
urban planning 4, 76, 84, 91, 116
urban politics
  bureaucracy and politics 78–96
  in developing industrial centres 61–76
  in early modern towns 52–6
  politics of class 131–3
  politics of consumption 9, 92, 129–30
  problems of representation 124–8
urban social movements 10
usurpation 28, 37, 42

Vancouver 17, 147–8
vestry 62, 65
Vipond, J. 98n

Waller, P. J. 74n
Wallerstein, I. 59n
Wates, N. 87n
Waterman, P. 143n
Weber, M. key features derived from 20–32
  on authority 27–8
  on bureaucracy 80–1
  on the city 32–50
  on class 29–30, 41, 50, 131
  on non-legitimate domination 37, 41
  on property 97–8
  on social action 25
Westergaard, J. 120n
Williams, G. 143n
Williams, R. 67
Wirth, L. 33
Wittich, C. 36n
Wohl, A. 62n, 74n

Wolff, M.   65n
Wolverhampton   73
working class   64, 72–6, 86, 96, 136
   consciousness   111
   division in   120
   and the Labour Party   124–5

Worsley, P.   13
Wrigley, A. E.   15n, 49n, 53n, 60–1

Young, K.   72n, 88, 91, 112

Zukin, S.   64n